T0148388

The Christs of God

George Cummings

iUniverse, Inc.
Bloomington

The Christs of God

Copyright © 2011 by George Cummings

All rights reserved. No part of this book may be used or reproduced by any means, graphic, electronic, or mechanical, including photocopying, recording, taping or by any information storage retrieval system without the written permission of the publisher except in the case of brief quotations embodied in critical articles and reviews.

The views expressed in this work are solely those of the author and do not necessarily reflect the views of the publisher, and the publisher hereby disclaims any responsibility for them.

iUniverse books may be ordered through booksellers or by contacting:

iUniverse
1663 Liberty Drive
Bloomington, IN 47403
www.iuniverse.com
1-800-Authors (1-800-288-4677)

Because of the dynamic nature of the Internet, any web addresses or links contained in this book may have changed since publication and may no longer be valid.

Any people depicted in stock imagery provided by Thinkstock are models, and such images are being used for illustrative purposes only.

Certain stock imagery © Thinkstock.

ISBN: 978-1-4502-8814-9 (sc)
ISBN: 978-1-4502-8813-2 (dj)
ISBN: 978-1-4502-8812-5 (ebk)

Library of Congress Control Number: 2011901447

Printed in the United States of America

iUniverse rev. date: 2/9/2011

Contents

To my children,
Karen, Kalaine, Richard, Jeffrey,
With gratitude for their love and affection

Introduction

I was the third of four children, two boys and two girls. I was jealous of my older brother and sister. They always seemed to be doing exciting things. But I have to admit now that when I got to do the same things, they weren't that great. As the third child, I learned from their mistakes about what could and couldn't be done.

I never knew my father very well. An Episcopal clergyman, he was forty years old when I was born. He died when I was seventeen. He was always busy with a large congregation in Richmond Hill, New York City, yet I can't recall discussing religion in the family. We took it for granted. I always knew my mother and father loved me and accepted me as a person. One particular incident comes to mind.

I attended public schools until the eighth grade. I was supposed to wait until the ninth grade to follow my older brother to an Episcopal high school; however, because I wasn't doing well as a student, my parents decided to move me to the private school a year early. It was a last-minute decision. The school year had already started. St. Paul's was a boarding school, but I attended as a day student. I went into the highest grade of the lower school. Since the other students knew one another from previous years, I found it hard to gain acceptance.

One day, the class waited outside the shop room for the master to unlock the door. There was a metal box with a key on a chain next to the door. The other fellows began to egg me on and tell me to take it from its rightful place. I didn't know what it was for, and I really didn't want the darn thing; however, I took it nonetheless. The next day was Saturday, and in the afternoon, when I was playing around the church with a couple of friends, my father called to me to ask if I had taken a key from the school. It was right there in my pocket, and I told him that I had. He said that we had to drive out to the school and take it back right away, because it was a key for the night watchman. He'd needed it the night before when he made his rounds.

It was a forty-five-minute drive. My father never asked me about what I had done, and I didn't offer any explanation. When we got to the school, I started to get out of the car, but he didn't make a move. I was surprised and asked, "Aren't you going with me?"

All he said was, "I didn't take the key."

I was left to face the headmaster, his assistant, and the head of the lower school by myself. I learned a lot from that experience.

I learned to take responsibility for myself and what I did whatever the consequences. I knew that my father suffered from my shame, because the school was part of the cathedral, the bishop of the Episcopal diocese of Long Island, New York, acting as chair of the trustees. At the same time, I realized my father supported me and accepted me as a person. It was not just because I was his son; he was treating me with respect as an individual. The sense of responsibility and individuality formed by that incident has stayed with me all of my life.

After I left home to attend the US Naval Academy, I continued being involved in the church. I taught Sunday school at the academy and continued to teach Bible study after I left the US Navy to work for Douglas Aircraft. Yet, I had to admit, I didn't know what Christianity was all about. More and more questions came to mind. I wasn't comfortable teaching children about things that happened according to the Gospels, which didn't seem to make sense in the world that I knew outside the church. I had a longing to find out for myself if there was something more to Christianity than I could see. I wanted some validation of the Christian faith. Finally, through the support of my wife and the help of my parish, I entered seminary. What an eye-opener!

Studying under one professor, Dr. Edward C. Hobbs, the professor for the study of the New Testament in Greek at the Church Divinity School of the Pacific in Berkeley, California, in the late 1950s and '60s, opened a world to me that I never knew existed, a world of the message that lay behind the stories of the Gospels and the writings of St. Paul. The first class with him was an incredible experience. It was like being a student pilot and suddenly reaching a stage on a solo flight where you feel that you are part of the airplane. It was the thrill of understanding the meaning of x squared or how logarithms worked or of seeing the significance and meaning of a masterpiece of art. Every class after that built on the first one.

At one point, I couldn't understand a comment he made about responsibility, and the two of us spent the entire class arguing as though there were no one else in the room. That was followed by a two-hour session in his office during which we went back and forth until I began to understand what he was talking about. He had been using the word "responsibility" in its root meaning of "being able to respond" and not in the more usual pejorative sense of "guilt." This understanding that there was more to the stories in the New Testament than met the eye was an illumination as well as one of my two major experiences of growth at seminary.

The other experience happened when I was working with Mrs. Harris, the voice teacher. I had the privilege of private tutoring with her the three years I attended seminary. She taught me how our emotions were revealed in the way we spoke and how to trust our instincts. It was a leap of insight for me, who had been trained with an engineering background in which everything was in black and white.

After I left seminary and became an ordained minister, I tried to share the fruit of these insights with others; however, I still wasn't able to get the message to my parishioners. I didn't have a grasp of how the bits and pieces of the writings of Paul and the Gospels fit together, not only with each other but also with the Old Testament and with life itself. I struggled for forty years to bring these insights and ideas into a coherent perspective with no real sense of success until recently when I conducted a Bible study class at the Cathedral Center of the Episcopal Diocese in Los Angeles.

I began that course of study with a great deal of trepidation. I had decided to try an entirely different approach. Instead of starting with an in-depth analysis of the Gospel of Mark, I began with an illustration of the problem we face, and without knowing it, I spoke about understanding the New Testament in terms of contemporary experience. I wanted people to see for themselves the relationship of the questions raised by the New Testament and the answers I had gleaned through the eyes of Dr. Hobbs. I proceeded in this way with a simple question that he had once raised in class about Levi, the tax collector, and I was amazed to see certain ideas fall into place. In particular, I asked how the Gospels were intertwined with the writings of St. Paul and the writings of the Old and New Testament Gospels, whose authors shared their understanding of the presence of God in their lives. I saw connections I had never fully understood before, ones which had not been covered by Dr. Hobbs. Equally surprising was the response from several people who participated in the class. One priest said that the course had changed his life.

With such encouragement, I put together the study of the Gospel message in order to share with others the enrichment that we shared in that study group together. Wasn't sharing enrichment what Christianity was all about after all? Sharing our lives of faith in response to the presence of God, not just within the fellowship of the church but with the world at large?

This study is designed to provide an understanding of the message of Christianity that underlies the intertwining of the writings of the Old and New Testament. The approach I take relies heavily on the Epistles of Paul and the Gospel of Mark.

I hope that, like the priest who believed his life had been changed, the lives of all who read this study will be changed as his and mine have been and as the lives of the early Christians were. I would hope that together we will see the presence of God in our lives as they saw it in their lives and that we will see the role that Jesus plays in the whole enterprise to the end that the glory of God might shine in us as it did in him and in those who followed him into the kingdom of God.

Academic Achievements

1. Graduated in 1961 from Church Divinity School of the Pacific in Berkley, California, with a master's degree in divinity and with honors in Theology and in Bible study.

2. Graduated in 1949 from the US Naval Academy with a bachelor of science degree in top 3 percent of the class.

3. Received in 1945 Pi Tau Sigma prize as highest ranking freshman in mechanical or industrial engineering and the Tau Beta Pi as the highest ranking freshman in engineering, at Lehigh University, Bethlehem, Pennsylvania.

4. Graduated cum laude in 1944 from St. Paul's School in Garden City, New York, where I was designated head student of the school in the junior and senior classes of 1943 and 1944.

Biblical Quotations

The biblical quotations in this book are based on the King James Version unless otherwise noted. The King James Version is closer to the Greek than other translations. Any translation of the Greek into English requires the translator to determine how best to pass on its understanding. Quotations will be adjusted to the common usage in the United States. There are also occasions when it isn't clear to whom a pronoun is referring. A reference to God will be capitalized as 'Him." The pronouns referring to Jesus are not to be capitalized.

A more serious problem is the Greek's minimal usage of the definite and indefinite articles (i.e., *a*'s, *an*'s, and *the*'s) and the lack of punctuation so essential in English. When these words are substituted for the Greek, they will be identified by italics. If they are used simply because of the nature of the English language, they will not be italicized. If the definite article is included in a Greek quotation, it will be identified by using italics for the definite article. The use of the definite article in Greek emphasizes the singularity of the following noun as in John 1:1: There is a significant difference between " a Son of God" and "the Son of God."

The source of the quotation will follow it in parentheses Example: (Goleman 2006, page 322). Reference to the chapter and verse of a quotation or a source will use the small letter "f" when there are two verses back to back. Example: (Romans 8:14f) indicating verses 14 and 15 make up the identity.

Chapter One

The Foundation

In Him was life and the life was the light of men (John 1:4).
That enlightens every man who comes into the world (John 1:9).

Around AD 40, in response to the preaching of Paul and Barnabas, the disciples of Jesus were first called Christians in Antioch (Acts 11:26). Their preaching gave a new meaning to the word "Christ." The word "Christ" is the Greek word for the Hebrew word "messiah," both of which translate into English as "the anointed one." The Jews applied the messiah title to a single individual anointed by God for a particular time to maintain, establish, or restore the kingdom of David. All the kings of Israel were the anointed ones.

In the Old Testament, an anointed one would be a king or a member of the temple hierarchy, such as a priest or a Levite. In the New Testament, Paul introduced an entirely different understanding of Christ. A Christ of God was anyone anointed with the life of God as an offspring of God whether or not the person was aware of being a child of God. Paul referred to the seed as the spirit of God when he wrote:

> Anyone led by the Spirit of God is an offspring of God, whereby we cry "Abba, Father." The Spirit bears witness with our spirit that we are the sons and daughters of God [as Jesus was]. *As God's children, we become* heirs of *the seed of God* and joint heirs with the Christ of God

1

> [in Jesus] so that together with him *we may show forth the glory of God.* (Romans 8:14–28)

The word "Christian" applied only to those who chose to be born again by being raised from the dead. We have to let go of the life we have been living in order to take on the life of God. We are then a Christ of God, just as Jesus was a Christ of God. Paul made that point in his comment: "My little children, of whom I travail in birth again until Christ be formed in you (Galatians 4:19). We die to the world into which we were born as we rise again to lead the life of God. The sacrament of baptism is a symbol of our death and rebirth.

John wrote about our being born again in the opening chapter of his Gospel:

> As many as received Him (God), to them gave He power to become the sons of God, even to them that believe on His name: *who are born*, not of blood, nor of the will of the flesh, nor of the will of man, but *of God*. And the *Word became flesh and dwelt in* us and we beheld his glory (in us), the glory as of an only begotten *offspring* of the Father, full of grace and truth. (John 1:12–14)

The above sentence has been changed to reflect the preceding verses (John 1:12-14) about our being born again by changing the word "among" to the word "in" and the definite article "the" to the indefinite article "an," John was following Paul's comment of the followers of Christ being born again.

God becomes our father only by our being begotten of God, just as Jesus became a child of God at his baptism. Being begotten of God is a never-ending choice we make by embracing the spirit of God as the spirit of our own being. When the translation uses the definite article "the" before "the only begotten son of the Father," it becomes a reference to Jesus alone, which is contrary to God's being our Father. To be His child, we *have to be begotten by Him.*

The Greek word translated as "among," is also misleading because it doesn't fit with the previous verse that said we are the children of God when we exercise the power God gives us to be born again.

The word translated as *"among"* is translated elsewhere as *"in"* in the New Testament 90 percent of the time. The comment that "the Word became flesh" with the words "dwelt *among* us" indicated that the flesh was Jesus and, therefore, "the only begotten Son of God." This doesn't make sense. The previous verse indicated that Christ was born in us as we chose to exercise the power given to us to have God. We then become God's offspring.

In his letters, St. Paul identified himself as a messenger commissioned to preach the Gospel of God. Paul based his understanding of the Gospel on the presence of God in our lives. According to the folklore story of Adam and Eve, God seeded Himself into Adam to make him a living soul. The seed was like a gene passed down from generation to generation, *enabling all mankind to become the living image of the Christ of God*. God is seeded in us, as He was seeded in Jesus.

According to Paul, our inheriting God as our Father defined the meaning of the word "Christ." Jesus became a Christ of God at his baptism, when the spirit of God descended upon him. God acknowledged him as His beloved Son by adoption, raising him from the dead. *Unfortunately,* the customary use of the word "Christ" considers it to be a reference to Jesus alone. Such understanding ignores the presence of the seed of God in every human being. Throughout this book, the word "Christ" is translated as "the Christ of God" or as "a Christ of God" as appropriate to stress the presence of God in our being His Christ Paul introduced this usage when he wrote the following:

> Don't you know that *you are the temple of God, and that the Spirit of God dwells in you?* You belong to God *as* a Christ because (by your living the life of God) Christ belongs to God (1 Corinthians 3:16, 23).

A New Heaven and a New Earth
(Isaiah 65:17; Romans 6:4, 7–6)

When we are living the life of God as His temple our understanding of the world around us changes dramatically. In the last century, our understanding of the world has changed. One of the characteristics of Paul's understanding about our world as Christians is that we are to walk in newness of light. No one can hold on to the past no matter how hard they try. We have more knowledge of the nature of the universe and of our humanity than any generation before us. Advances in understanding the nature of how our brains work through genetics and computerization alone have changed our lives almost beyond comprehension.

With a newly installed a hundred-inch mirror telescope on Mt. Wilson in 1925, Hubble discovered the universe was expanding. This meant the universe is changing moment by moment, day by day. We are always moving into a new universe. Before this discovery, most astronomers and physicists believed the universe was as it always had been and would continue to be so. The Milky Way was thought to be the only galaxy in the universe, existing forever as it was. Hubble discovered two dozen more galaxies. Today, we know there are billions of galaxies. Hubble also discovered that the more distant galaxies were moving away at an increasing speed, indicating the universe was expanding. By 1929, the significance of his discovery became apparent. It changed our understanding of the universe. What I read indicates Hubble deduced pretty much by himself with his colleagues (who go unnamed)

The expansion of the universe meant the universe was smaller yesterday than it is today. The day before yesterday it was smaller than yesterday, and so on until we reach a point of beginning in the form of an infinitesimal dot which contained every thing that exists. The universe and every thing in it has been in a constant state of change as it continues to expand. In every instance, there is a new universe. Every existing thing in the universe has a past. Time began when the dot exploded in a massive burst of electromagnetic energy known as the Big Bang. *Every thing in the universe has a beginning in the Big Bang. Every thing that exists traces itself to this event* (Isaacson 2007, 353–5). Most people are familiar with this theory, which is self-evident in the discovery of the expansion of the universe.

As the energy expanded into space, it cooled and slowed down. The energy developed into masses of particles, which clumped together to form galaxies of stars, planets, and even black holes. These masses of matter are burning energy, which sustains their existence. Some of the energy becomes unrecoverable heat known as entropy. According to one theory, expansion will continue until entropy gradually cools to the absolute zero of outer space. The universe and everything in it will then be subsumed into empty space whence it came (Wikipedia, Title: Big Bang).

Mankind has long been searching for the answer to the question, "Why do we and the universe exist?" When this question was put to Stephen Hawking, he replied, "If we knew that, it would be the ultimate in triumph of reason, for we would be looking at the mind of God" (Wikipedia, Title: Time). St. Paul addressed the question with an answer based not on reason but on his experience of God's grace on the Road to Damascus coupled with his knowledge of the Bible, which had been gained through years of study begun in early childhood. Paul wrote of the mind of God with regard to Jesus's being in the form of God:

> *Let this mind be in you which was also in Jesus, a Christ of God*, who, being found in the form of God, did not count it as robbery *to be equal with God*. (It was a gift.) (Philippians 2:5f)

Because every existent thing traces itself back to the big bang and because we are the only things with a mind that can understand anything, the source of everything has to have a mind far more capable than ours. From a scriptural standpoint, the universe and everything in it is an expression of the mind of God.

The folklore story of Adam and Eve in the Garden of Eden explained how human beings came into being on "the day [eon] when God created the heaven and the earth" (Genesis 2:4). The story was written around about 2500 BC (Wikipedia, Title: Eden Story). In his letter to the Romans, Paul wrote how the mind of God became the destiny of our humanity:

> Who has known the mind of the Lord God? Of Him and through Him and to Him are all things. May He be glorified forever. I beseech you to present yourselves as living sacrifices. Do not be conformed to this world but be transformed *by the renewing of your mind so that you may prove what is the good, acceptable, and perfect will of God*. Through the grace given to me, I say to everyone, do not think of yourself more highly than you ought to think. Let love be without dissimulation. Abhor what is

5

evil. Cleave to what is good. Be kindly affectionate with one another with brotherly love. Do not be slothful, but be fervent in spirit, serving the Lord God. Rejoice in hope. Be patient in tribulation. Continue instant in prayer. Bless those who persecute you and curse not. Be of the same mind with one another. Recompense to no one evil for evil. If it is possible, as much as you can, live peaceably with everyone. Be not overcome with evil, but overcome evil with good. (Romans 11:34, 36; 12:1–21)

The six-day story, which preceded the Garden of Eden story in the Bible, was written about 350 BC, when Judaism was exposed to the astrological discoveries in Greece and Babylon, to explain how God created the heavens and the earth. The story led into the story of Adam and Eve. In the six-day story, God created everything by His spoken word, indicating the universe was the expression of God. The story culminated with the decision to *make mankind in God's image*, for them to "be fruitful and multiply, to fill the earth and subdue it, and to have dominion over every living thing" (Genesis 1:1–2:3). Through the advances in theoretical physics we have come to understand a great deal about the basic characteristics of the universe in which 'we live and move and have our being' (Acts17:28)According to the discovery made by Albert Einstein, space is essential to the propagation of light (Isaacson 2007, 318). The physical qualities of space enable light to transmit the power of the sun to our whole solar system. Light also carries information which has led to the understanding of how *gravity is the property of space as it* accommodates the presence of matter. The physical qualities of space reveal themselves in its interaction with matter and with the electromagnetic forces of light.

Prior to these announcements, Einstein explained how his general theory accounted for the attraction between masses of matter, which caused them to clump. To illustrate the clumping, he used the image of a bowling ball placed in the middle of a trampoline and billiard balls on the outer edge of the trampoline. The hollow caused by the weight of the bowling ball attracted the smaller billiard balls. This image (referred to as a "warping of space-time") implied that the contact point of space-time with matter is in one spot on a piece of matter. Actually, the *gravitational force of space encapsulates itself around matter, clumping and holding the masses together.*

In my estimation, a better image for the action of gravity as a property of space shows the action as a series of fishnets encapsulating the mass, one net atop another putting pressure on the mass from all sides. When the outer nets of the gravity field of one mass interact with the outer nets of another mass, the inner nets between the two masses meld together. The inner nets cancel each other out. The outer nets of both masses push the masses together into a clump.

Without the clumping of space, there would be no universe. Furthermore, without space, there would be no medium for the propagation of light. (Isaacson 2007, 318).

The Light of Understanding
(Romans 13:12)

When light strikes an object, the atoms absorb the energy carried by light. Now in a higher energy state, the atom emits photons with the same wavelength as the atom's frequency spectrum. Every element in the universe has a particular frequency spectrum of light. The spectrum of an element is like a fingerprint or a signature. It identifies the elements that make up a star, for example.

Aborbed light is not emitted as a wave. The photons are emitted in a particular direction like a stone thrown from a sling. Directed light defines the size and shape of any object we can see. The light emitted from the atom is not a reflection. It is an emission from the atom itself. For example, if the light from the moon were a reflection of light received from the sun, we would not be able to see the moon. The surface of the moon would act like a mirror reflecting the sunlight just as we see ourselves in the reflection of a mirror. We would see the sun reflected from moon's surface. The light we see comes from inside the atoms of whatever object we can see (Isaacson 2007, 322–7).

Light enables us to see whatever is going on around us. Other information comes to us from the senses of sound, taste, smell, and touch. This information about our situation relies on the visible section of the brain to form images of what we see. The human brain is the distinguishing nature of our humanity. Everything we do is decided in our minds. We are the only entities able to understand, to think, and to reason. The capacity of the human brain far exceeds the capacity of our nearest primate, whose neurons are measured in the millions. We have a hundred billion neurons in our brain with a trillion connectors (Goleman 2006, 150). On the other hand, our genes differ from the primate's by only 3 percent. Without the capacity of our brains, we would be little different from a chimpanzee or an orangutan (Wikipedia, Title: Human Brain vs. Animal).

Understanding, however, is more than thinking. It involves making images in our brain of how people and things behave in their interactions with one another, how they situate and enact their being in relation to one another. The imaging process of understanding is an essential part of everything we think and do. Our ability to create images in our minds is a process by which our retinas turn the energy of the photons into electricity, which become an image of what we are seeing in the visible section of the brain. *Light is the basis of our understanding ourselves, our interaction with others and with the things within the world. Blind people use different senses to create pictures, such as touching, hearing, smelling.*

Everything we say, think, see, hear, smell, or touch is kept in our memory banks so that we are able to recognize the situation in which we find ourselves. When information comes to our brains about what is going on around us, the brain evaluates whether or not the situation is a threat. If it is a threat, such as the breaking of a heavy branch overhead, a snap decision is imaged for our immediate response. If it is a familiar situation, we respond subliminally as we have in the past. In the case of unfamiliar situations, we have to work our way through perhaps two or three options imaged out of past experiences in our memory banks. Consider the following example. You have guests coming for dinner and suddenly remember that you have forgotten to pick up the cake you ordered at the bakery. You rush out to your car, turn on the ignition, and start to back out, but the car sputters to a stop then. You try the ignition again. It sputters but doesn't keep running. You say to yourself, "What's going on?" You get a little upset, which prompts you to look at your gauges, and you discover you are out of gas. You say to yourself, "You forgot to get gas yesterday."

You go on talking to yourself, "Good grief! How am I going to get gas? I could call the AAA as I did the last time I ran out of gas, but it took them an hour to get to me. Wait a minute. The gas station is only a couple of blocks down the street. I could walk down and get some gas. Uh-oh, I have to get a can to bring it home. Hey, I have a can of gas for the lawn mower. Oops, it's a mixture of gas and oil in the portion of fifty to one. I wonder if it will work." Sure enough, you get the can and pour in the gas tank. The engine starts, and you are on your way. What a relief.

As you have read this out-of-gas experience, you have followed along, imaging yourself in the situation as well. You experienced some sense of the emotions involved, beginning with annoyance for forgetting to get the cake, followed by frustration over the car not working because you forgot to fill up on gas. In your mind, you saw yourself in the snags cropping up until you got to the surprising elation of the fifty-to-one mixture powering the car. While you read the example, your brain treated your imaging involvement as though you had actually gone through it, even though it was an imaginary experience.

This scenario has been sent to your memory bank as a "have-been" experience available if something similar happens to you in the future. In the next few weeks, if you run out of gas or if you see your gas gauge come close to empty, this scenario may come up in your mind and prompt you to stop for gas. The memory bank of have-been experiences is essential to understanding. Without that bank, we would have no have-been experiences to begin the process of projecting ourselves forward to deal with whatever is ahead of us. The history of who we have been is an important part of our being who we are now.

When we choose a particular optional image developed in our minds to deal with an unusual situation, our minds activate our muscles to carry out the action. Making that choice reveals the self we are bringing into being. The sense of the self we choose to be is the "I" of whatever we are doing. When we choose a particular option, we immediately put it into action. Our "I" expresses the "am-ness" of our being in the action we choose to take. This experience gives us a sense of what we mean whenever we use the word "I." Our "I" is the emotional control center directing the "am-ness" of the self we are bringing into being in any instance of our lives. Our "I" makes itself known in the process of considering the various options presented. Our "I" is not a material thing. It is a pocket of emotional energy. The "I" we choose to be depends on the emotional state of our minds. An angry or frustrated parent will choose a different self than a parent who cares for the well-being of the child (Goleman 2006, 14).

The Mind of the Universe

We have already seen how the scientific discovery of the expansion of the universe led to our understanding that everything traces itself back to the big bang. We cannot see beyond the big bang, because it marks the beginning of time. We do not have instruments to go back beyond that beginning; however, two aspects of the source of the dot and its explosion into space as the electromagnetic force of light reveal the physical effects of space.

Space warped to accommodate the dot as a gravitational singularity under tremendous pressure, which increased its temperature to unmanageable heights and ultimately led to the big bang's explosion. Space acted as an ether, a medium for the propagation of light. Space was the source of the dot. Without the clumping effect of gravity, there could be no universe. Without a medium of space for the propagation of light, there would be no transfer of energy to keep the universe working. Without light, we could not explore the universe.

As a thing of this world like everything else, our mind has a past tracing back to the source of everything that exists. The story of Adam and Eve is a story much like theoretical physics. It is only a folklore story tracing our history back to the beginning of the universe in the same way theoretical physics traces the beginning of the universe back to the big bang. Both rely on tracking our existence back through time to the beginning of time. Its message reveals itself when we look beyond the written word.

The story of Adam and Eve is the seminal story for everything in Judaism and Christianity. That story revealed God as the source of everything in the universe. Later, in answer to Moses's question about his name, God answered, "Yahweh," which most English translations render as "I am that I am." Moses was to say to the people, "'I am' sent me." The Greek Bible (Septuagint) renders the translation of Yahweh as "I am the being," and Moses was to tell the people, "'The being' sent me." The Greek translation suggests everything that has being is an expression of God (Septuagint, Exodus 3:14). Paul put it this way: "The invisible things of [God] from the creation of the world are clearly seen, being understood by the things that are made, even His eternal power and Godhead" (Romans 1:20). John opened his Gospel in similar fashion:

> In the beginning was the Word and the Word was with God and the Word was God. All things were made by Him, and without Him was not anything made which became existent. (John 1:1, 3)

The Eden story (Genesis 2:4-24) goes on to reveal God clumping clay and water together and forming it into man. Then He breathed Himself into man to bring man into being. He put man in the Garden of Eden, instructing him to care for it. God went on to warn man about eating of the Tree of Knowledge of Good and Evil, because if man did, "he would surely die." Then God said, *"It is not good for man to be alone."* With these words, God revealed the emotional state of His mind in creating Adam. He was concerned for Adam's well-being. If it was not good for man to be alone, then it was not good for God to be alone. God shared Himself with mankind. God went on to make Eve in the same image as Adam. She was "bone of his bone, and flesh of his flesh." Adam had someone in his own likeness with whom to share himself. The emotional state of God and humankind is to care for the well-being of everyone and everything in the universe.

God's care for Adam and Eve continued after they failed to obey His warning not to eat from the Tree of the Knowledge, for if they did, "they would surely die," and they did die. *They died to the life of God.* However, God did not take away the self He had sown in them when He inspirited His own self in Adam. God continued to care for them. He provided them with animal skins to cover themselves. *God also left His life in them in a dormant state as a seed to be awakened if they turned to God.* He expelled them from the garden to guard them from access to The Tree of Eternal Life. If God left them to themselves, alienated from His life as they were, they could have eaten of The Tree of Eternal Life, locking themselves into an eternal life without access to the self of God. God did not take away their experience of His presence as the self they could be. To live the life of God, they had to die to the life of alienation from being as God was (Genesis 3:21–24).

Chapter Two

High and Low

Choosing to Be

Once Adam and Eve tasted evil, the experience was with them forever in their minds' memory banks. It was passed on from generation to generation. According to recent neurological discovery, two roads live in our memory banks today, one called the "high road" and the other the "low road" (Goleman 2006, 13–7).

The "low road" operates "slam and bang," as in "act first and think afterward." It cares only for its own well-being with little or no thought of those around them. The low road leads to careless bondage in the environmental 'they' world, into which we are born. In the carelessness of the low road, we only consider ourselves or our families or the ones in our own social, economic, political, religious, educational world. Our behavior in the 'they' world is guided by the current fad with the excuse, "Everyone does it." We are in bondage because 'they' determine how we are to behave (Goleman 2006, 16). The 'they' world has no self of its own. We are mired in the "been there, done that" of the past.

The "high road" leads to our brain's executive center, which contains our capacity for intentionality (the will of our being), such as carefulness (Goleman 2006, 16). Choosing the road of carefulness takes more time. Our memory banks have to consider everyone and everything involved in whatever situation we find ourselves. In the scriptures, the carefulness road is called the road of righteousness. It leads us to bring into the present the future will of God—carefulness for the well-being of ourselves, those nearby, and the universe itself.

These two options gain strength through usage. We have to choose who and how we are going to be. The availability of choosing the life we will follow is found in the book of Deuteronomy:

> The word of God is not in heaven that you should say, 'Who shall go up for us to heaven, and bring it unto us, that we may hear it, and do it? Neither is it beyond the sea, that you should say. Who shall go over the sea for us and bring it unto us so that we may hear it and do it?' The word is very near unto you, in your mouth and in your heart that you may do it… I have set before you life and death, blessing and cursing; therefore choose life, so that both you and your seed may live. I have set before you this day life and good, death and evil. (Deuteronomy 30:12–15)

St. Paul paraphrased Deuteronomy about the presence of God in our lives as opposed to the dead life of alienation from the mind of God in his first letter to the Corinthians:

> Who shall ascend unto heaven, to bring the Christ of God down? Or, who shall ascend into the deep to bring up the Christ of God again from the dead? The word is nigh you, even in your mouth, and in your heart: that is the word of faith. (Romans 10: 6–8)

The Resurrection of the Dead

Paul's experience on the road to Damascus led him to understand that seeking righteousness by the law is self-righteousness. Paul wrote that the righteousness of God comes to us as a gift: "[Jesus] died for all, so that they which live should not live unto themselves but unto him who died for them and rose again. Anyone being in the Christ of God is a new creature. Old things are passed away, all things become new" (2 Corinthians 5:15, 17).

To walk in newness of life, we have to let go of our old way of life. In Paul's mind, letting go of the old life means dying to that life. For Paul, sin is failure to live the life of God: "All have sinned and fall short of the glory of God" (Romans 3:23). At our baptism, we are buried with the Christ of God as we die to the life we have been living. *We are raised to the new life of righteousness, which shines from within us as the glory of God, just as Jesus rose from the dead, the life of Judaism at his baptism:*

> As in Adam all die (when he and Eve ate the forbidden fruit) so in the Christ of God shall all be made alive. Do you not know that as we were baptized into Jesus, a Christ of God, we were baptized into his death? We are buried with him by baptism into death so that, like as the Christ of God was raised from the dead by the glory of the Father, so we also should walk in newness of life. *Since we have been planted* [seeded] in the likeness of his death, we shall also be in the likeness of his resurrection. (Romans 6:3–5)

> For God, who has caused the light to shine in darkness, has shined in our hearts to give the light of the glory of God in the face of Jesus. (2 Corinthians 4:6)

Paul's reference to death is not a reference to our demise (Ephesians 5:14). *Death for Paul is alienation from the life of God. We are then dead to the life of God.* Our death is like Adam's, who lived nine hundred years after eating of the Tree of the Knowledge, in that we, too, go on living a life alienated from God. To live the life of God, we have to be raised from the dead. The resurrection can only happen to a living human being. We are to "walk in newness of life" (Romans 6:4).

> You are our epistles of the Christ of God written not with ink, but with the Spirit of the living God; not in tablets of stone, but in the fleshly tablets of the heart. By God's grace, the Christ of God has made us a minister of the new covenant; not of the letter [of the law, the 'they'

world of Judaism], but of the spirit; *for the letter kills, but the spirit gives life* … If the ministration of death [the law] written and graven in stone was glorious, so that the children of Israel could not behold the face of Moses, much more does the ministration of righteousness [the life of God] exceed in glory. But now you are delivered from the law, *being dead wherein we were held, so that we should serve in newness of spirit and not in the oldness of the letter.* (2 Corinthians 3: 2–8; Romans 7:6)

The law does not bring death by itself. Death under the law comes when obedience to the law is the measure of our righteousness. Obedience to the law is meaningless unless it is based on concern for the well-being of others. All transgressions of the law have been forgiven by the life and death of Jesus. "Whoever loves another has fulfilled the law. Love, (as care for another), is the fulfilling of the law" (Romans 13:8–10).

You, being dead in your sins [unrighteousness], [God has] made you alive together with [the Christ of God], *having forgiven you all trespasses blotting out the handwriting of ordinance* [the law], *and took it out of the way by nailing it to the cross.* (Colossians 2:13–15)

According to Paul, walking in newness of life happens to us now in this life. "Now is the acceptable time; now is the day of salvation" (2 Corinthians 6:2). We are raised from the dead as we let go of the old life to walk in newness of life. Paul's comment reflected both Isaiah's declaration about our salvation and Micah's description of what it means to walk in newness of life:

In an acceptable time have I [God] heard you and in a day of salvation I have helped you. I will preserve you and will give you as a covenant for the people … What does the Lord require of you, but to act righteously, to show mercy [forgiveness] and to walk humbly with your God. (Isaiah 49:8; Micah 6:8)

The glory of God is planted in us as seeds for us to cultivate and grow in the likeness of the Christ of God. Our dying to sin allows the seed to take root and grow to be a tree of righteousness producing fruits of righteousness (Romans 6:22), Isaiah identified the seed as the word of God by which God expressed himself:

> As the rain and snow water the earth and make it bring forth and bud, giving seed to the sower and bread to the eater *so shall my word be.* It shall not return to me empty, but it will accomplish my pleasure and prosper in whom I send it. You shall go out with joy and be led forth in peace; the mountains and hills will break forth before you into singing and the trees of the field will clap their hands … The spirit of the Lord is upon me; he has anointed me to preach the Gospel…to comfort all who mourn, to give them beauty for ashes, the oil of joy for mourning, the garment of praise for the spirit of heaviness, so that will be called trees of righteousness, *the plantings of the Lord,* and be glorified [with his life]. (Isaiah 55:10–12; 61:1, 3)

Paul paraphrased Isaiah, connecting his comments with the six-day story of creation about our destiny to be "fruitful and multiply":

> Now, [God who] ministers seed to the sower, thereby ministering bread for your food, and multiplies your seed sown, and increases the fruits of your righteousness. (2 Corinthians 9:10; Philippians 1:11)

The seed and the bread of the self of God dominated the stories in the four Gospels. They were the basis of the parables about the seed falling on various kinds of ground (Mark 4:3–30; John 12:23–27); the two feedings of the multitudes in the wilderness (Mark 6:35–45; 8:1–21); the disciples' harvesting and eating wheat on the Sabbath (Mark 2:23–28); the healing of the Syrophenician's daughter about the dogs eating the crumbs of bread that fell from their master's table (Mark 7:24–32); Jesus's cursing of the fig tree (Mark 11:12–14) for not bearing fruits of righteousness (Luke 6:43); and the blessing of the bread and the wine at the Lord's Supper (Mark 14:22–25).

Paul's comment about the seed planted in us refers to it as a brain cell similar to a gene. The brain cell carries the likeness of our predecessors in this case, producing the glory of the life of God. Such a cell could well be called the "God cell." Paul traced the seed back to the faith of Abraham in his comment, "The promises were made to Abraham and *his seed*, which is the Christ of God" (Galatians 3:16).

There are two possibilities: We are either the offspring of God as the Father of righteousness, or we are the children of the fickle world into which we are born (Romans 12:2) and reject the gift of God's eternal life. When we are under the control of 'they,' we have no sense of responsibility for the way we are. Nobody is at fault because "everyone does it." We blame everything that goes awry on ' 'they' who is everybody and nobody. 'They' change with every whim and fancy and fad that comes down the pike.

As children born of God, we are free to choose who we will be in every situation we find ourselves. We become responsible for ourselves in choosing life or death. Paul refers to our being in the 'they' world as being asleep, quoting Isaiah, who wrote, "Arise, shine; for your light is come and the glory of the Lord, is risen upon you" (Isaiah 60:1). Paul put it this way:

> Awake, you who are asleep and arise from the dead and the Christ of God shall give you light. (Ephesians 5:14)

> Now it is time to awake out of sleep ... night is far spent, the day is at hand, let us therefore cast away the works of darkness and put on the armor of light. Put on the Lord Jesus, a Christ of God, and make not provision of the flesh to fulfill the lusts thereof. (Romans 13:14)

The light of the Christ of God sets us free from bondage to the works of darkness. Our future is set free from the past. We are "fore-given" (as the word used to be spelled). We are "given a new future," a new "fore." In the "covetous world, we don't have a future. We live for a "Been there, done that" experience. We become part of an "in" group that we have found attractive. Living in the past without a future is being dead to the life of God. Paul put it this way:

But now we are delivered from the law, that being dead wherein *the law* being dead when we were held so that we should serve in newness of spirit and not in the oldness of the letter. (Romans 7:6)

Servants and Messengers of the Resurrection

Paul and the other Gospel authors shared their experience of the life of God. The words "according to" in the titles of the Gospels indicate their work was based on their individual experience. Like Jesus and Paul, they were resurrected from the dead to become servants of righteousness in newness of spirit:

> Reckon yourselves to be dead unto sin, but alive unto God through Jesus, a Christ of God, our Lord. Being made free from sin we become servants of righteousness [by choice]. You have your fruit unto holiness and the end, everlasting life. You become dead to the law by [being] the body of the Christ of God so that you are married to one another, even to him [the self of God] who raised you from the dead so that you bring fruit unto God. Now we are delivered from the law, [since we] are dead wherein we were held [by the law] *so that we can live in newness of spirit* and not in the oldness of the letter of the law.
>
> Our old man is crucified with [the Christ of God]... [Anyone] dead [to the life of sin] is freed from sin. You have your fruit unto holiness [righteousness] and the end—everlasting life [of God]. The wages of sin is death but the gift of God is eternal life through Jesus, a Christ of God, our Lord ... serving [God] in newness of spirit. (Romans 6:6–11, 18, 23; 7:4-6)

Paul changed the meaning of sin. Until his Damascus road experience, Paul, like all Jews, understood sin to be failure to obey the written word of God in the law of ordinances and commandments.

19

Following his experience, Paul came to understand sin as failure to be as God is. Sin is living in the ungodliness and unrighteousness of the selfish 'they' world. (Romans 1:18; Psalm 14). Paul went on to write the following:

> The righteousness of God has been revealed by the faith of Jesus, a Christ of God. All who have sinned *under the law* and fall short of the glory of God are made righteous by His grace through the redemption of the Christ of God *in* Jesus. God set him forth to be a propitiation through faith in his blood for the remission of sins of the past *under the law*. (Romans 3:21–25; 4:24)

Rising from the dead differs from resurrection. A resurrection means there was a previous rising. The word for resurrection translates into Greek as "raised again." Paul made that point in his letter to the Corinthians: "I delivered to you first of all what I received, how the Christ of God died for our sins according to scripture and how he rose again the third day according to the scripture" (Hosea 6:2: 1 Corinthians 15:1–4).

Jesus rose from the dead at his baptism when the spirit of God descended on him and he became a Christ of God, as an offspring of God. Three days after his crucifixion, the Christ of God in Jesus was resurrected (raised again) in the disciples. All resurrections from the dead have to be a bodily resurrection, because, as we have already seen, the word "Christ" means a human being anointed with the life of God. Every raising of the Christ of God after Jesus's baptism is a resurrection. Every rising of the Christ of God in us is a dying to the self we have been. We have to die to one life to take on a new life. Paul also made this point when he wrote about presenting ourselves as living sacrifices:

> I beseech you to present your bodies as living sacrifices, holy and acceptable to God, which is your expressional [the expression of God] service ... and be not conformed to this world, but be transformed by the renewing of your mind, that you may prove what is the good and acceptable and perfect will of God. (Romans 12:1f)

Paul had the same experience of sacrifice and resurrection on the road to Damascus. At his baptism, he gave up his dead life of obsession to obedience of the law in the same way Jesus was raised from the dead life of righteousness by the law. God calls us, too, to rise from the dead like Jesus and Paul.

Choosing to live the life of God is not a one-time event. We often fall back into the befuddled 'they' world. We continuously have to renew our minds. Our failings are forgiven even as we fall into them. God gives us a new chance to choose again to be resurrected with Christ of God. Paul expressed his surprise at God's forgiveness on his trip to Damascus. He saw himself struggling against God. God not only forgave Paul. He also called him to preach the Gospel of God (Acts 9:1–21; Romans 1:1). Paul made this point with his comments about his "dying daily" (1 Corinthians 15:31) and his "delight for the law of God" (mercy and forgiveness) while at the same time aware of ungodliness within him (Romans 7:18–24). In the face of failure to hold on to the life of God, he yet "pressed on for the prize of the high calling of God in Jesus, a Christ of God" (Philippians 3:7–14).

Failure to live the life of God like any other kind of mistake is a learning experience. In the act of failure to be as God is, God forgives us. He continues to offer the option of being a child of God. To press on, we have to accept God's forgiveness as we again die to the 'they' world. That is what it means to walk in newness of life. We don't like to admit we failed. We would rather live in the 'they' world and blame the nonexistent 'they' as the ones—parents, teachers, peers, or the government. Paul faced himself in his failure and did a complete turn around, embracing the life of God. After his baptism, he went into the desert to consider what was happening to him. He came to understand how his obsession to seek righteousness by the law destroyed him. Paul saw he had been pulling himself up with his bootstraps, bragging about how he was more zealous "for the traditions of the fathers than the equals around him" (Galatians 1:14). In the process of examining his failure to achieve righteousness through the law, Paul came to understand the significance and meaning of the life of God in the life and death of Jesus. Paul's knowledge of scripture enabled him to write the "Gospel of God concerning the life of Jesus" (Romans 1:3).

Who Covered First Base

The arrangement of the books of the New Testament is misleading. In the New Testament, the four Gospels and the Book of Acts precede Paul's letters, suggesting his writings were based on the Gospels. Just the opposite is true. *The four Gospels are based on the writings and preaching of St. Paul.*

The listing of the Gospels is out of order. Mark wrote the first Gospel around AD 66, followed by Luke, Matthew, and John, each separated by about ten years. Mark set the stage for the others to follow. Mark was a protégé of St. Paul. Paul began to preach the "Gospel of God" around AD 39. He wrote his epistles from AD 50 to AD 60. Both of them based their Gospels on the writings of the prophets in the Old Testament. The New Testament was not about the life of Jesus per se. The New Testament described Jesus's life and death as the fulfillment of the prophecies of Isaiah and Jeremiah.

Paul and Mark opened their Gospels with references to the prophecies of Malachi and Isaiah (Romans 1:1; Mark 1:1), both of whom have a common theme about the New Covenant. Malachi prophesied that God would appear in His temple, which would be the messenger of the covenant, rising as "the Sun of righteousness with healing on his wings" (Malachi 3:1; 4:2). Isaiah, whom God anointed ("christed" in the Septuagint) to preach good tidings (Isaiah 60:1), prophesied God would annul the covenant of death made by Israel (Isaiah 28:15–18). God would give His suffering servant as a covenant of the spirit to heal both Jews and Gentiles. God's servant would bear the iniquities of Israel by His torture and death as a sacrificial lamb (Isaiah 42:6; 49:3–8; 53:3–12).There would be a new heaven and a new earth (Isaiah 65:17). Paul and Mark described the suffering and death of Jesus in the same way Isaiah described the suffering and death of God's servant (Isaiah 52:13–53:12; Romans 5:6–9; 6:10; Mark 15:15–28).

Paul's introduction in his letter to the Romans led the way for Mark's opening of his Gospel with quotations from Malachi and Isaiah. Paul wrote the following:

> Paul, a bond servant as of Jesus Christ of God [one anointed with the life of God], called to be an apostle, commissioned to preach the Gospel of God, which was

written by His prophets beforehand in Holy Scriptures, concerning his son Jesus, a Christ of God, our Lord, who was born of the sperm of David with regard to the flesh, and declared to be a Son of God by the power of the Holy Spirit's resurrecting the dead. (Romans 1:1–5)

Mark opened his Gospel in much the same way:

The beginning of the Gospel of Jesus Christ, the Son of God, as it is written in the prophets, Behold I send my messenger before your face, to prepare the way before you, the voice of one crying in the wilderness "Prepare you the way of the Lord, make straight in the desert a highway for our God." (Mark 1:1f)

Paul and Mark indicated their preaching and writings were based on the writings of the prophets in the Old Testament. The New Testament authors wrote about the Christ of God being revealed in themselves in keeping with Paul's experience. They, too, saw themselves "called to be apostles." They, too, were cast into the role of Malachi's messenger of the covenant, in whom God would appear (Malachi 3:1; 1 Corinthians 15:5–9). In Greek, the word "apostle" means "one who is sent with a message."

Paul went on to say Jesus was "declared to be the Son of God according to the spirit of holiness which came by the resurrection of the dead" (Romans 1:4). The resurrected dead were those raised to live the eternal life of God radiating from the life of Jesus, from Paul himself, and from the other people resurrected from the dead. They became the sons and daughters of God just as Jesus became an offspring of God at his baptism, because it was then that he received the Holy Spirit. Jesus's title as the Christ of God referred to his preeminence as the first human in the history of mankind to reveal the life of God (Colossians 1:18).

The presence of the Holy Spirit in a person's life is evidence of living the life of God. If the fruits of the Holy Spirit do not radiate from a person's life, then that person is dead to the life of God. Paul wrote of his dying to the ruthless 'they' world when he wrote, "I am crucified [dying to the 'they' world] with the Christ of God; yet I live, but it is not I who live, but the Christ of God who lives in me" (Galatians 2:20).

Mark wrote of a similar statement made by Jesus: "Whoever shall come after me, shall deny himself [the uncaring 'they' world] and take up his cross and follow me. For whosever will save his life [in the 'they' world] shall lose it; and whoever shall lose his life [in the 'they' world] for my sake and the Gospel's shall save it [as spiritual life]" (Mark 8:34f).

Messengers of God

The Christ of God was resurrected in the lives of those close to Jesus as they died to the 'they' world, following in Jesus's footsteps. We, too, are called to be Christs of God following in Jesus's footsteps, dying to the 'they' world. "Don't you know that when we were baptized into the Christ of God in Jesus, we were baptized into his death to the law?" wrote St. Paul. "We are then buried with him by baptism into his death, so that as the Christ of God was raised from the dead by the glory of the Father, we, too, should walk in newness of life in the likeness of his resurrection" (Romans 6:3–23).

When the Christ of God is raised in us, we become the body of the Christ of God in our generation, as were Jesus, Paul, Mark, Luke, Matthew, and John in their generations. The New Testament writers shared their lives in the Christ of God with us so that we, too, might be resurrected into the life of God in the fellowship of the daughters and sons of God through the Christ of God in Jesus. When the Spirit of God appears in us, we are the Word of God just as Jesus was the expression of God in human form (John 1:14).

The beginning of life as a Christian starts with the resurrection from the dead. Our will becomes God's will then. Our mind becomes God's mind. We become the messengers of the New Covenant for the befuddled world around us.

Messengers of the New Covenant stimulate the God gene in others. The stimulation makes itself known in the options of caring for the life of everyone and everything. That is how God calls us to be born again, raised from the dead into the life of God. We are called by the grace of God to be His suffering servants and messengers, equal with Jesus, Paul, and the other writers of Holy Scripture. We have more understanding of the nature of the universe and of our humanity than any generation before us. This scientific knowledge not only correlates with the Gospel message but also sheds light on our understanding of the message in our time.

The Image of God

When we choose to be transformed into the image of God's life as the Christ of God, we become the human form of God's being. The will of our life becomes the will of God's life. We, then, are Isaiah's plantings of the Lord as trees of righteousness bearing fruits of the Holy Spirit. In the form of God, we come into synchrony with the mind of the universe:

> Let this mind be in you, which was in the Christ of God, Jesus, who, being in the image of God, thought it not robbery to be equal with God, and took upon himself the form [image] of a servant and humbled himself and became obedient to death, [suffering] even death on a cross. (Philippians 2:5–8)

> I beseech you therefore, brethren, to offer yourselves as living sacrifices [dying to the past to live the life of God], holy and acceptable as your Godlike service of his word. Do not be conformed to this world, but be transformed by the renewing of your mind so that you may prove [for yourself] what is the good and acceptable will of God. (Romans 12:1f)

> Put off the former behavior of the old person [you have been] with its corruption in deceitful lusts. Be renewed in the spirit of your mind. Put on the new person [the Christ of God] created of God in righteousness and true holiness. (Ephesians 4:22)

When Paul encouraged us to choose to take on the mind of Jesus, a Christ of God, he used the term "the Christ of God" to mean the mind and the spirit of God. The latter was the emotional state of God's mind driving His interaction with everyone and everything in the universe. Suffering the death of our old self is the sacrifice by which we become servants of God's being. We have to die to the 'they' world to live the life of God. According to Paul, Jesus is not the only "Christ of God." He makes this clear with such comments as the following:

- You are the body of the Christ of God (1 Corinthians 12:27).
- Let the word of the Christ of God dwell in you (Colossians 3:16).
- Your body is the temple of the Holy Spirit (1 Corinthians 6:19).
- All who are led by the spirit of God are the offspring of God (Romans 8:14).
- I live, yet not I, but the Christ of God lives in me (Galatians 2:20).
- Be renewed in the spirit of your mind and put on the new man (Ephesians 4:23f).
- Put on the Lord, Jesus, aChrist of God (Romans 13:14; Galatians 3:27).

Throughout this book, the word "Christ" has been used with the definite or indefinite article to emphasize our individuality as the Christ of God. When we put on the Lord, Jesus, a Christ of God, we are born of God, anointed with the Christ of God—the life of God revealed in Jesus's life and death. We then "live and move and have our being, in God" (Acts 17:28) as offspring of God (i.e., seeds of God), a daughter or son of God, just as Jesus was a Son of God. How does our brain work for us to live, move, and have our being in the mind of God? The answer lies in the emotional state of our minds in the everyday way we live and move and have our being.

Sharing Emotions

Neuroscience has made remarkable discoveries about the sharing of emotional feelings between individuals:

> [The brain] reads the emotional aspect of whatever we perceive—elation in someone, tone of voice, a hint

of anger around the eyes, a posture of glum defeat—
and then it processes that information subliminally,
beneath the reach of conscious awareness. This reflexive,
unconscious awareness signals that same emotion by
priming the same feeling in those nearby—a mechanism
for catching a feeling from someone else. When we
are near another person, the circuitry of that person's
emotion primes itself in us, appearing as an option for
us to choose. In order to reach sharing and consonance,
we have to trigger that primed self. We then emit the
other's emotion. We have to let go of ourselves [or the
other person has to let go of him or her self] for both to
be on the same wavelength. (Goleman 2006, 15)

Goleman goes on to quote Daniel Stern's observation: "Our nervous
systems are constructed to be captured by the nervous systems of others
so that we can experience others as if from within their skin. At such
moments we resonate with their experience, and they with ours," sharing
emotions in consonance with the other's brain cells (Goleman 2006,
43).

In the case of someone stubbing a toe, crying out, "Ouch," and
writhing on the ground in pain, those nearby will feel the pain and be
faced with choices of an emotional response, such as an offer of help,
"Are you all right? Do you need any help?" or sympathy, "Oh, that hurt,"
or annoyance, "Why don't you watch where your going?" All but the
one who is annoyed indicates a caring emotional state of resonance with
the injured person.

We also share the emotional state of animals the same way we read
the emotional state of humans. A dog playing fetch has an emotional
effect on us that is different from the emotional effect of a dog chewing
on a bone and growling when we get near him. Weather, seasons, and
climates have a beneficial or a frightening effect on our emotions, too.
Inanimate things have an emotional effect on us as well. Standing at the
foot of the El Capitan (that huge granite outcropping of three thousand
feet in Yosemite Park, California) or on the rim of the Grand Canyon
in Colorado fills most people with an emotional sense of awe before the
nature of the universe.

Our emotional interaction with other humans, animals, and inanimate objects is a face-to-face experience. It is a case of "I see you smile, and I smile," or "I see you get angry, and I get angry." Our brains emit electromagnetic waves of energy. Neuroscience has been able to harness the energy. In one case, they have been able to wire the motor section of a paraplegic's brain to a computer connected to an artificial hand, enabling the paraplegic to control the hand just by thinking about it.

Daniel Stern's observation about our experiencing the mind of others "as if under their skin" comes from the light emitted from a person's face. The light conveys the emotional state of that person's "I." In most instances, the light primes the circuitry of the same emotional state for us to choose for ourselves. We don't have to choose the other's feelings. In the case of charismatic individuals like Jesus or Paul, their emotional state was so powerful that it triggered the emotional state of mind of the Christ of God in others nearby them. This phenomenon of transmitting our emotional state to others underlies Paul's statement about the glory of God shining from the face of the Christ of God in Jesus:

> God, who commanded the light to shine in the darkness,
> has caused the light to shine in our hearts to give us the
> light of understanding the glory of God in the face of
> the Christ of God. (2 Corinthians 4:6)

When we put on the Christ of God, we become transmitters of His mind. We become messengers of the light of understanding, "the invisible things of God, clearly seen by the things that are made, namely His eternal power and deity" (Romans 1:20). Paul wrote about his experience on the road to Damascus when he saw the option to be the image of the Christ of God in Jesus. Paul spoke of himself as "one born out of time" (1 Corinthians 15:8; see also John 3:1–15.) He had been born a second time as an adult, raised to a third heaven (2 Corinthians 12:2), where he saw indescribable things. (1 Corinthians 2:10–16)

Every thing emits the light of God's being, but only humans can understand the scope and meaning of the emotional state of His being. We are the only things that exist with a brain capable of understanding anything. This doesn't mean that animals can't sense the emotional state of the circumstances in which they find themselves and act accordingly. Owners who emit the emotional state of leadership easily train dogs, but dogs' brains, as with other mammals, are not capable of thinking through various options. They simply don't have the brainpower to think, mainly because they don't have a language. They can communicate limited bits of information with one another through sound and movements of various kinds, but their response is instinctive because of evolution and/or training. Their choices in unusual situations are to flee, fight, or freeze.

Evolution of Benevolence

As we have already seen, the Eden story of creation reflected an understanding of the spirit of God—the benevolent emotional state of care for all—as the driving emotional force of our humanity and the universe. The biblical stories of creation set the theme of understanding the nature of God. They run from the beginning to the end.

From Genesis: "The spirit of God moved over the waters and God said, 'Let there be light.' The Lord God formed man of the dust of the ground and breathed into his nostrils the breath of life" (Genesis 1:2; 2:7).

To Isaiah: "Arise, shine, the glory of your light has come, and the glory of God is risen upon you, and the Gentiles shall come to your light" (Isaiah 60:1, 3; 2 Corinthians 4:6).

To the Christ of God in Jesus and in Paul: "Knowing, now is the time to wake out of sleep. The day is at hand. Put on the armor of light [of understanding]; put on the Lord, Jesus, the Christ of God" (Romans 13:11, 14).

To the Christ of God in Jesus in the Gospel of John: "In Him, the Word of God made flesh, was life, and the life was the light of man ... which enlightens every man that comes into the world" (John 1:4, 9).

To John's vision of the end: "I, the Alpha and Omega, the beginning and the end, will make all things new ... a new Jerusalem descending from heaven, having the glory of God and her light clear as crystal. There shall be no night and no need of a candle or the light of the sun for the Lord gives [His servants] light" (Revelations 21:6, 10; 22:5; Isaiah 65:17).

Isaiah's prophecy, "The glory of God has risen upon you," led to a dramatic change in man's understanding of God. God would replace Moses's covenant of the *law* with a covenant of the benevolent spirit of God (Isaiah 59:21). God would gather all nations and tongues to see His glory and to worship before Him (Isaiah 66:18–24). God's house would be a house of prayer for all people (Isaiah 56:6). In Paul's words, we would become Isaiah's house of prayer for all people, the temple of God, the body of the Christ of God, and the dwelling place of the Holy Spirit (1 Corinthians 3:16; 6:19; Romans 8:9).

Those who live by the spirit of the glory of God are the children (the offspring, the seed) of God (Romans 8:14). On the one hand, living by the letter of the law kills. On the other hand, living by the spirit of the glory of God is the fulfillment of our destiny as human beings (2 Corinthians 3:6). If this is true, the information available through genetics, theoretical physics, neuroscience, archeology, geology, and anthropology should indicate how our brain evolved to provide us with the option of choosing to live the life of God.

Goleman described the evolutionary circumstances within which care for the well-being of others would develop as a trait of the human race:

> Our natural pull [care] toward others may trace back to the conditions of scarcity that shaped the human brain. We can readily surmise how membership in a group would make survival in dire times more likely, and how being a lone individual competing for scarce resources with a group could be a deadly disadvantage. A trait with such powerful survival value can gradually fashion the very circuitry of the brain, since whatever proves most effective in spreading genes to future generations becomes increasingly pervasive in the genetic pool. (Goleman 2006, 56)

Ice cores reveal such a dire time of scarcity during the eruption of the Toba Volcano in Sumatra seventy-three thousand years ago that marked the beginning of an ice age lasting another thousand years The eruptions spewed sulfur particles into the air, which crystallized and blocked out the sun for ten years. An ice age was about to begin, and the absence of sunlight exacerbated the effect of the ice age, giving it a head start. Most of the earth was covered with ice after that.

The world population of Homo sapiens was reduced to between one thousand and ten thousand breeding pairs. This reduction, known as "the bottleneck of evolution," was just above the extinction line and fits well with genetic information available today. All human beings living today trace their lineage to our most recent ancestors living sixty thousand years ago in the male gene and a hundred thousand years ago in the female gene. Prior to that, sophisticated tools and other artifacts from between seventy-five thousand and fifty-five thousand years ago suggest language had advanced during this period so that humans could teach children and others how to use and make the tools for survival.

Prior to the bottleneck, the survivors lived in small tribal bands within various territories, eking out an existence in contention with other tribal neighbors. The bottleneck decimated the individual tribes, leaving fewer people necessary for the tribe's survival. When they met survivors of other tribes, they approached each other with mixed emotions of trepidation and hesitation. They were used to fighting with one another. When they overcame the fear of previous confrontations of fight, anger, and revenge, they worked together for survival in friendship and cooperation, relying heavily on their emotion of compassion, concern, and kindness. The survival of each individual was essential for the group to survive. Care for the well-being of others became a fundamental characteristic of our humanity (Goleman 2006, 56). Recent research into the functioning of our brains reveals two sections in the frontal area where unique neurons produce a sense of self-awareness not only of our selves but also of those nearby. These sections lie at the center of our brains where social emotions, such as empathy, trust, guilt, jealousy, embarrassment, love, kindness, and concern develop. "Self-awareness and social awareness are part of the same functioning, and these neurons, known as von Economo cells, are part of that process" (Goleman 2006, 38).

Goleman writes of care as empathy, too. He describes it as becoming aware of another person's feeling and responding to the other's distress or happiness (Goleman 2006, 58). Paul speaks of care as charity later, often translated as "love":

31

> Though I speak with the tongues of men and of angels [messengers] and have not charity, I am become as sounding brass, or a tinkling cymbal. Charity suffers and is kind; charity does not envy, charity does not vaunt itself, is not puffed up. Does not behave itself unseemly, seeks not her own; is not easily provoked, thinks no evil. Now abide these three: faith, hope and charity, but the greatest of these is charity. (1 Corinthians 13:1–5, 13)

Unlike charity, love is more often understood as an emotional state of mind apart from any action. On the other hand, charity, based on care for the well-being of everyone and everything, is accompanied by acts of kindness and compassion. The emotional involvement of charity initiates action to help people we see in some difficulty, distress, pain, danger, need of help, or elated mindset. We see ourselves in their situations. We feel for them and bring into our minds how we would feel in similar circumstances. The compassionate act may be a kind word, a smile, a listening ear, or just time near them to give encouragement and to let them know there is someone to help and care for their well-being or perhaps even share their joy with them.

From Birth to Adulthood

Neuroscience research has found that people with the mindset of caring for the well-being of themselves, of those nearby, and of the environment in which they find themselves live longer (Goleman 2006, 370). They have healthier lives than most do because of an accompanying strong immune system. Sharing the emotional state of others develops a sense of well-being and results in the sense of fulfillment. They seldom get stressed out. Jesus was such a person, as were his followers, Paul and the other writers of the New Testament. In his comment about charity, Paul described its development with this observation:

> When I was a child, I spoke as a child, I understood as a child, I thought as a child, but when I became a man, I put away childish things. (1 Corinthians 13:11)

When a child is born, one third of the hundred billion neurons in a mature brain have already developed. These neurons control the functions of our vital organs. Another third of the neurons develop by the age of two. The final third are almost complete at the age of twelve, with most of their self-control neurons in place. By the age of twenty-five, all the self-control neurons are in place (Goleman 2006, 152).

The first two years of a child's life are the most critical years for the development of his or her behavioral circuitry. In the first two years, the child's mind is like a sponge, soaking up everything that is going on around it. By the age of two, the child will be able to walk and talk in a basic way. Unlike the other neurons that begin to form at birth, self-control neurons, essential to our ability to project ourselves into different ways of being, don't begin to develop until the age of the "terrible twos." If these self-control neurons start to develop much later than two, they may not develop sufficiently. Not until the age of twelve do these self-control neurons mature to the time when a child can begin to take responsibility for he or her choices. However, full maturity of the self-control neurons does not develop until the age of twenty-five.

Self-control neurons, along with our memory bank, are essential to becoming the caring people that our minds are designed for. Self-control neurons are designed to impose a time delay before we take any action. Without them, we would make instinctive, snap decisions much like the state humans were in before this genetic adaptation. The self-control neurons impose an instant delay so that we can consider the situation and what action is best. The next time you get angry, think back to the beginning of it, and you will find there was a split second when you decided to get angry (Goleman 2006, 15–17).

The self-control neurons are meaningless without the memory bank of have-been experiences. The memory bank neurons are the source for the images into which we project ourselves. They develop as we learn how to act in familial, social, economic, and political environments.

The family environment determines a child's development of a sense of responsibility. Children who are given opportunities to do things on their own within their capabilities at every age, with compassionate guidance and discipline, feel sure of themselves in changing circumstances (Goleman 2006, 154–65). Every child needs to find out how far he or she can go at a particular age. On the other hand, families whose parents and siblings fly off the handle at the drop of a hat, who lose control, who take advantage of one another, and who play favorites breed the same responses in children.

With a strong self-control development, children are more likely to avoid being sucked into following the pack just to belong. Discipline given with care and compassion is important. Yelling at anyone is a put down and only triggers the same emotional response. Until the age of twelve, a child has little control of him or herself. He or she is told what to wear, when to bathe, when go to bed, how to brush his or her teeth, when get a haircut, what words are acceptable, and which aren't. Then at the age of twelve, the child suddenly becomes responsible for his or her behavior.

Such responsibility comes at a time when the child is about to go through the dramatic change of puberty. At that age, the child is going to be thrown into a new school situation, namely high school, where a child's main concern is fitting into a new environment. Because the child is coming from a long period of looking to others for the rules of the road, he or she will now look to older students, who are not inclined to give the best advice. The child moves from the familial world to the beguiled world, where no one is in control.

As we have already seen, the self of the 'they' world is nobody and everybody. It is the composite mixture of where the action is, of what new excitement might give meaning to life. When we are living in the dead 'they' world our inner "I" feels at odds with its genetic self of caring for the well-being of everything—for ourselves, those nearby, and the environment around us. We just don't feel right.

The 'they' world has the advantage of time and energy. In the 'they' world, we spend much less time and energy deciding what we want to do, because 'they' have already decided what is appropriate. We avoid the responsibility of ourselves, because we let someone else make the decisions for us, often with the excuse, "everybody does it." On the other hand, the "caring world" takes time and effort to think through a situation and all the factors involved, with consideration not only for ourselves but also for others and the environment affected by our actions. The 'they' world is around us all the time, enticing us with its emotion of self-absorption, driving us into the future without care for others and the surrounding environment.

Chapter Three

From Birth to Adulthood

The Gospel of God According to Paul

We grow up thrown into a world not of our own choosing. We learn a language and how to behave in the environment into which we are born. In time, just when our bodies are producing all kinds of hormones, we are supposedly ready to take control of ourselves. We become aware of the uniqueness of ourselves when we are faced with choices. When we realize our failings, we make excuses, deny our responsibility, and blame others for our missteps. Choosing to be a "caring person" is not easy. Paul referred to his own struggle to do the right thing when he wrote:

> When I would do good, evil is present with me. For I delight in the law of God [carefulness] after the inward man; but I see another law in my members, warring against the law of my mind and bringing me into captivity in the law of sin... O wretched man that I am; who shall deliver me from the body of this death? I thank God through Jesus, a Christ of God, our Lord. (Romans 7:21–25)

Paul's struggle developed out of his family environment. He was the right person in the right place at the right time. Born into a wealthy family, he was under the tutelage of tutors and sages at an early age. He could speak Greek and Hebrew. His family was full of devout Jews who instilled in Paul an obsession to "seek righteousness" through the law. At about fifteen or sixteen years of age, Paul went to Jerusalem to study under Gamaliel, the foremost Pharisaic sage of the time (Acts 22:3). Paul proved to be "above my equals: more zealous of the traditions of my fathers" (Galatians 1:14). Paul's dedication to Judaism led him to persecute those known as "the People of the Way of Holiness." He was responsible for the death of many of them. Paul sought letters from the high priest authorizing him to seek out any followers of "the Way" in the synagogues of Damascus (Acts 9:1f; Galatians 1:13).

Paul's trip to Damascus was a dangerous undertaking (Hosea 6:9). The five- or six-day trip covered some a hundred and fifty miles. Travelers joined together for protection against highwaymen. On the way, Paul spent time thinking about how he would persuade the synagogues to reveal suspects. He came to see that these were devout Jews following the way of righteousness based on the baptism of repentance for the forgiveness of sins, which was preached by John the Baptist (Mark 1–4). Jesus had assumed leadership of John's followers after his execution at the hands of Herod Antipas about 26 BC.

As Paul neared Damascus, he realized their response to John the Baptist's call to repentance for the forgiveness of sins by the cleansing of baptism was based on a sense of the inadequacy of temple sacrifices and burnt offerings as a means of atonement for ungodliness. Repentance isn't just turning toward God. It is also a turning away from ungodliness. Temple worship didn't do the job. Repentance to the followers of John meant obedience to the law. Jesus became the leader of John's followers after John's death. John's followers lived the life of God emanating from Jesus, thinking that their sense of fulfillment was due to obedience.

After Jesus's crucifixion, they sensed the presence of God as they followed in Jesus's footsteps. Without realizing what was happening to them, they followed both John's preaching and the life of God in Jesus. They continued to be called "the People of the Way," measuring righteousness by the law while at the same time actually living the life of God as they followed in Jesus's footsteps.

Paul had spent his life studying the law to achieve righteousness by obedience to the law. All his endeavors in pursuit of obedience and

understanding of the law failed to give him a sense of righteousness
(Philippians 3:4–8). He had studied scriptures since his childhood. He
recognized "the People of the Way" were following Isaiah's highway of
holiness (Isaiah 35:8). He needed only to think of other Old Testament
writings about how God regarded temple worship:

> Hosea (2:18–19; 6:6): In that day I will make a covenant
> with them [says the Lord God]. I will betroth them to
> me in righteousness, and faithfulness. I desire mercy
> not sacrifice, the knowledge of God more than burnt
> offerings.

> (Isaiah 1:11–16; 2:5) Shall I come before [God] with
> burnt offerings? Will the Lord be pleased with thousands
> of rams, or with ten thousands rivers of oil…What does
> the Lord require of you, but to do righteously, and to
> love mercy, and to walk humbly with your God?

> Micah (6:7): To what purpose is the multitude of your
> sacrifices to me … I am full of the burnt offerings…
> Bring no more vain oblations… Your appointed feasts
> are hateful to me … *Wash you, make you clean*, put away
> your evil doings from my eyes…Come and walk in the
> light of the Lord.

Paul's thoughts on the trip to Damascus may well have brought a
painful remembrance of his first exposure to "the People of the Way."
He had not only witnessed the stoning of Stephen, but he had also
given his consent and had held the garments of the stoners (Acts 8:1).
His persecution of "the People of the Way" was often on his mind. As
he came in sight of Damascus, he saw himself persecuting the seed of
God in Jesus and in "the People of the Way" (Acts 9:3–6).

The experience changed his life. Paul sought out the leaders of "the
Way" in Damascus to be baptized. His conversion occurred about 39
AD. He went off into the desert to understand the significance of his
experience in the light of his vast knowledge of the Old Testament.

When he returned to Damascus, he preached the Gospel of God
(Romans 1:1) for years until he was forced to flee the city. His message

so upset the Jewish community that they planned to kill him. He sought out the early followers of Jesus in Jerusalem to join their community. His former persecution of "the People of the Way" upset some of the Grecian converts to Judaism, and these converts planned to kill Paul. The community of Jesus's followers would not accept Paul, and they sent him to Tarsus (Acts 9:27–30).

The stoning of Stephen led some of the followers of "the Way" to flee from Jerusalem. Some settled in Antioch and preached about "the Way." The Jerusalem community sent Barnabas to Antioch, where his preaching urged many people to become "People of the Way." Barnabas then found need of Paul and brought him to join in preaching the word in Antioch (Acts 11:19–30). After three years, he and Barnabas went to Jerusalem with an offering to help the community. In meetings with Peter, James, and John, they all agreed that Peter would be sent to the Jews while Paul and Barnabas would preach to the Gentiles (Galatians 2:1–8).

Jesus's followers had assembled in Jerusalem, the religious center of Jewish worship, in anticipation of the establishment of the kingdom of God. They lived in a commune governed by twelve disciples with James, the brother of Jesus, at its head, acting in counsel with John, the son of Zebedee, and Peter, who were both the pillars of the community.

They spoke of Jesus as "the messiah," the anointed one, the individual destined to restore the political kingdom of Israel as it was in the time of David. They continued to follow the law and observed the various feasts with their accompanying sacrifices but also with a sense of repentance.

The Chronology of the Message

The word "Christian" was first used in Antioch around AD 42 in response to the preaching of Paul and Barnabas. The name suggested the followers of the Christ of God in Jesus considered themselves to be born of the Christ of God (Galatians 4:2–12; 1 Corinthians 15:8). Adherence of the early Jerusalem community to the law was Paul's nemesis (Galatians 2:12). The community sent representatives to stir up followers of Paul in the various cities Paul visited. The Jewish followers of "the Way" in various synagogues resisted Paul's preaching about the

Gentiles, whom they insisted could not be followers of the Christ of God. The Jewish people of "the Way" would not eat with them unless they were circumcised (Galatians 2:11; 6:12).

Paul and Barnabas made a trip to Jerusalem to discuss the situation. They obtained letters releasing the Gentile converts to Christianity from the requirement of circumcision so long as they obeyed the major ordinances of the law, namely "abstention from pollutions of idols, and from fornication, and from things strangled, and from blood" (Acts 15:1–21).

Paul viewed the law as ordinances of man. Paul wrote to the Galatians, "Man cannot achieve righteousness by works of the law, but by the faith of the Christ of God, Jesus. The just shall live by faith; the Christ of God has redeemed us from the curse of the law so that we might receive the promise of the Spirit through faith" (Galatians 2:16; 3:13). He goes on to say, "All the law is fulfilled in one word, 'You shall love your neighbor as yourself. If you are led by the spirit, you are not under the law'" (Galatians 5:14, 18; Leviticus 19:18).

Paul's reference to the curse of the law is found in Deuteronomy 21:23: "Cursed is everyone that is hanged on a tree" (Galatians 3:13). In Paul's preaching, the Christ of God's death on the cross set Christians free from the law. The Christ of God's death replaced not only the law but the Old Covenant of Moses with a New Covenant prophesied by Isaiah (49:8), Jeremiah (31:31), and Hosea (2:18, 23).

The New Covenant

The Jerusalem community of "the Way" was true to Moses's covenant. Their fathers committed themselves to the covenant by a sacrificial rite in the wilderness. In the wilderness, Moses gathered the people together for the reading of "all the words he had received from God" (Exodus 24:1–11). Then "Moses sprinkled upon the people the blood from peace offerings of oxen and said, 'Behold *the blood of the covenant* which the Lord has made with you'" (Exodus 24:8). The peace offering of oxen was shared between the people and with God. The people ate the meat while God received the smoke from the burning fat. The establishment of the New Covenant included the body and blood of the Christ of God.

In his first letter to the Corinthians (10:1–21), Paul reviewed the experience of the Jews in the wilderness with regard to their commitment to God. In doing so, Paul revealed the significance and meaning of the two rites practiced throughout Christianity, namely Baptism and the Lord God's Supper. He connected baptism with the release from bondage by a commitment to repentance, letting go of the 'they' self and taking on the self of God revealed in the life of Jesus. Paul then connected the Lord God's Supper to the spiritual nourishment of the body and blood of the life of God in Jesus, strengthening and encouraging Christians to fulfill our commitment to live the life of God. At the Lord's Supper, we feed on the self of God in communion and fellowship with other like-minded people attending the rite. Paul's words speak his mind:

> Our fathers were under the cloud, and all passed through the sea…All were baptized in the cloud and the sea … All did eat the same spiritual food … and did drink the same spiritual drink, for they drank of that spiritual Rock that followed them. That rock was the Christ of God. (1 Corinthians 10:1–4)

> The cup of blessing we bless, is it not the communion of the blood of the Christ of God? The bread which we break, is it not the communion of the body of the Christ of God? For we being many are one bread, and one body: for we are all partakers of that one bread … are not they who eat of the sacrifice partakers of the altar? You cannot drink the cup of the Lord, and the cup of devils; you cannot be partakers of the Lord's table and of the table of devils. (1 Corinthians 10:16–19, 21)

In the next chapter, he goes on to establish the Lord God's revelation of Jesus's words at the Lord God's supper on the basis of his previous comments about the bread and the wine:

> When you come together in the church, there are divisions among you. This is not the Lord God's Supper. On the other hand, Paul wrote "I have received of the Lord God … that the Lord Jesus, on the night he was

betrayed he took bread: And when he had given thanks, he brake it and said, 'Take, eat, *this is my body*, which is broken for you: this do in remembrance of me.' After the same manner also he took the cup, when he had supped, saying, "This cup is the New Covenant in my blood, this do, as oft as you shall drink it, in remembrance of me." (1 Corinthians 11:23–25; 2 Corinthians 6:14)

The New Covenant dominated Paul's thinking. In his second letter to the Corinthians, he had this to say about the New Covenant in relation to the law and the spirit:

> [God] has made us able ministers of the New Testament [covenant], not of the letter [the law], but of the spirit, for the letter kills, but the spirit gives life. (2 Corinthians 3:6; Jeremiah 31:31–34)

In his letter to the Romans, Paul connected the New Covenant to Isaiah's description of its nature: "There shall come out from Zion the Deliverer. For this is my covenant with them when I take away their sins" (Romans 11:26; Isaiah 60:14). Isaiah wrote of the deliverer as the suffering servant whom God would "give as a covenant to the people" (Isaiah 59:20):

> The Spirit of the Lord will lift up a standard [the cross] … and the Redeemer shall come to Zion, and unto them that turn from transgression. This is my covenant with them: my spirit that is upon you, shall not depart [be withdrawn] from your mouth, nor from your seed's mouth, nor your seed's seed. Arise, shine, for your light is come, and the glory of the Lord is risen upon you. The darkness shall cover the earth but the Lord shall arise upon you and his glory shall be seen upon you. And the Gentiles shall come to your light, and kings to the brightness of your rising (see Mathew 2:2, 11). You shall know that I, the Lord God, am your Savior and Redeemer. (Isaiah 59:19–60:3, 16)

Jeremiah made the same prediction of the presence of God based on forgiveness of sin:

> I [God] will make a new covenant. I will put my law in their inward parts and write it on their hearts…and they shall no longer teach [one another] to know the Lord for they shall know me from the least of them to the greatest … for I will forgive their iniquity and will remember their sin no more. (Jeremiah 31:31–34)

Both Jeremiah and Isaiah indicated the New Covenant occurs when we are cleansed of our transgressions and ungodliness. In Paul's understanding, cleansing came when the Christ of God in Jesus died on the cross for our righteousness, giving "Himself for us, an offering and a sacrifice to God" (Ephesians 5:2):

> By his stripes we are healed [cleansed] … The Lord has laid on him the iniquity of us all … He was brought as a lamb to slaughter … He was cut off from the land of the living … For the transgression of my people was he stricken. My righteous servant shall justify [make righteous] many; for he shall bear their iniquities. (Isaiah 53:1–12)

Isaiah also connected the cleansing and healing of the cross with rebirth and resurrection in the Greek translation of the Hebrew Bible, the Septuagint, which was the Bible of the Christian followers of Paul. Isaiah, when he wrote the following:

> Your [God's] chastening [cleansing] was to us with small affliction; and, as a woman in travail draws nigh to be delivered and cries out in pain, we have conceived, O Lord. We have brought forth the breath [spirit] of salvation. The dead shall *rise*. Those in the tombs shall be raised. The dew from you [washing] is healing to them. (Isaiah 26:16–19)

Like Isaiah, Hosea and Malachi also connected the resurrection with the healing of the cross in response to God's chastening, turning us away from being dead in ungodliness:

Come let us return to the Lord, for he has torn and
he will heal us. He has smitten and he will bind us
up. After two days will he revive us. In the third day
he will resurrect us and we shall know him. (Hosea
6:1–3) (In the *Septuagint,* the Greek word is the same
word translated in the New Testament as the verb to
resurrect.)

Unto you, who revere my name, *shall the Sun of
righteousness arise with healing on his wings.* (Malachi
4:2; Mark 1:10)

Hosea's prophecy was the source of Paul's knowledge he received
from God, that knowledge containing the fact that the resurrection
would take place on the third day as he says in the following passage:

For I delivered unto you that which I received, how
that the Christ of God died for our sins, according
to the scriptures; and that he was buried, and that he
rose again according to the scriptures. (Hosea 6:2;
1Corinthians 15:3)

In writing to the Galatians, Paul was adamant that God revealed
to him the Gospel he preached. God revealed the Christ of God in him
on the road to Damascus. Paul even said the following:

I certify to you, brethren, the Gospel, which was
preached of me, is not after man. For I neither received
it of man, neither was I taught it, but by the revelation
the Christ of God in Jesus. When it pleased God … to
reveal the Son in me … I conferred not with flesh and
blood. The things I now write to you, behold, before
God, I lie not. (Galatians 1:11–20)

The Messengers of the Covenant

Paul's letters began with an introduction of himself as a messenger, "a
bond servant as of the Christ of God in Jesus, called to be an apostle,

43

commissioned for the Gospel of God, which he had promised beforehand in the Holy Scriptures" (Romans 1:1). The word "apostle" means "one who is sent with a message." Paul described Jesus as the temple in whom God would appear as the messenger of the covenant in fulfillment of the prophecy of Malachi. Paul's message cast Jesus in the role of Isaiah's suffering servant, who died for our iniquities.

Paul also wrote of Jesus as the healing covenant of Hosea (2:18) and the heartfelt covenant of Jeremiah (31:31–34). Paul saw himself and all the apostles who followed in Jesus's footsteps as the temples of God, carrying in themselves the message of the New Covenant wherever they went.

Chapter Four

Beyond the Written Word

The Message behind the Words

As the messengers of the New Covenant, it is critical that we understand the message we are to carry into the world. The Gospels are different from the writings of St. Paul. It is difficult to imagine Paul and the authors of the Gospels were writing about the same thing. In this regard, St Paul never referred to a miracle Jesus performed. Furthermore, except for Jesus's words at the Lord's Supper, Paul never quoted a statement attributed to Jesus in the Gospels. The apostles did not agree with one another, particularly in the first three Gospels of Mark, Luke, and Matthew. For example, Mark and Luke referred to the kingdom as the kingdom of God, while Mathew wrote of it as the kingdom of heaven. John wrote of the kingdom only five times: twice as the kingdom of God and three times, in a statement of Jesus, a Christ of God, as "my kingdom." The theme of John's Gospel was eternal life. John included only a few details from the first three Gospels. Each Gospel followed the lead of its predecessors.

Some of the healing miracles don't make sense, suggesting there is more to the stories than meets the eye. In the story of the paralytic (Mark 2:1–12), how could the people, packed together in the room with Jesus, avoid injury when the paralytic's friends dug a hole in the roof above them? In the story of the demoniac of the Gadarenes (Mark 5:1–

19), what was a herd of two thousand pigs doing in Israel? How could a woman with an issue of blood for twelve years survive without bleeding to death (Mark 5:25–34)? What did Jesus expect the disciples—and us—to understand when He rehearsed the numbers of the people fed, the loaves of bread, and the baskets of fragment in the two feedings in the wilderness (Mark 8:13–21)? Reading beyond the words of these and other statements in the Gospels will help reveal their connection with the epistles of St. Paul.

As already noted, of the four Gospels written after Paul's letters, Mark's was the first in AD 66. Consider the situation Mark faced at that time. The persecution of "the People of the Way" led to the death of James and probably Peter in AD 62. Mark had probably recently learned of Paul's death in the persecution of Christians, which followed the burning of Rome in AD 64. Nero had blamed the Christians for the fire and ordered a persecution of them throughout the empire. At the same time, Israel was in the early stage of rebellion against the Roman forces occupying their country. Between Nero's persecution and the turmoil in Jerusalem, the early community of "the Way" fled from Jerusalem to Pella on the northeast side of the Jordan above the Sea of Galilee.

Mark was the one most familiar with the history that led to the crucifixion of Jesus. Mark was raised in a household where the early fellowship of "the People of the Way" met (Acts 12:12). He was probably about four or five years old when Jesus was crucified. He would have been fourteen or fifteen when his uncle, Barnabas, took him and Paul to Antioch and included him in their first journey to preach the Gospel. Mark left them after their first two stops in Cyprus.

Much later, around AD 58, Mark joined Paul again when Paul was in prison for two years at Caesarea before he went to Rome. Mark was originally called John. After he changed his name from John to Mark, he became a student and follower of Paul's preaching, which probably alienated him from his family, who were committed to the covenant of Moses as people of "the Way." The same alienation may be said of Paul with regard to his family. Paul never mentioned his family, even though he passed through Tarsus more than once. The objection of their families to their change of heart may lie behind the story of Jesus family's attempt to stop his ministry (Mark 3:31–35).

Mark was with Paul when he wrote most of his epistles while under house arrest in Caesarea around AD 60. Mark made a trip to Ephesus at Paul's request to get copies of Paul's epistles dispersed among the churches around the Aegean (Philemon 1:24; Colossians 4:10; 2 Timothy 4:11). Around this time, Paul wrote he had "fought a good fight, and finished his course" (2 Timothy 4:7). He intended to go to Rome and then to Spain. He needed the books and parchments for reference (2 Timothy 4:13). He knew he probably would not be returning to the near East.

Mark may have been moved to write his Gospel because of the paucity of information in Paul's letters about the life of Jesus. Paul never quoted anything Jesus said, except for the revelation of his words at the Last Supper, which came to him by revelation from God. Without Jesus, there would be no letters of Paul or word "Christian." Paul is the one who first came to understand the meaning of the life and death of Jesus as it was written by the prophets. He spent his life studying the Bible. He consummated his formal study of the Bible under Gamaliel in the four or five years prior to his experience on the road to Damascus. He wrote of his credentials in his letter to the Galatians:

> I certify to you, my brethren, that the Gospel which I preached did not come to me from man. I was taught it by the revelation of the Christ of God in me. I studied the Jewish religion beyond my equals, being more zealous to learn the traditions of our fathers, It pleased God to call me by His grace to reveal His Son in me that I might preach about him among the heathen. I went to Arabia and then returned to Damascus. Then after three years I went to Jerusalem to see Peter for fifteen days. (Galatians 1:10–17)

According to Acts 9:23, Paul spent "many days" in Arabia, which probably means he spent a year. Paul came to grips with the significance of his Damascus experience. Without Paul, there would be no New Covenant, no sacrifice for our iniquity, no words of the Lord's Supper, no resurrection from the dead life of ungodliness (sin). He wrote the following:

> Now if it be preached that Christ rose from the dead, why do some of you say there is no resurrection of the dead (raising from the self centered world, alienated from the life of God)? But if there be no resurrection of the dead, then Christ is not risen. If Christ is not risen then my preaching is meaningless and your faith is vain. (1 Corinthians 15:12–14)

The four Gospels are about the Christ of God in both Jesus and Paul. The Gospels entwined the lives of Jesus and Paul. This entwinement became apparent in the opening words of Mark's Gospel and of Paul's letter to the Romans. Both of them are messengers of the Covenant.

> The beginning of the Gospel of Jesus, a Christ of God [one anointed with the life of God] as it is written in the prophets: "Behold, I send my messenger before your face, who shall prepare the way before you; the voice of one crying in the wilderness, 'Prepare you the way of the Lord, make his paths straight.'" (Mark 1:1–3; Romans 1:1; Malachi 3:1, 4:5; Isaiah 40:3)

The Fulfillment of Holy Scriptures

Mark indicated he was going to write about the beginning of the Gospel of Jesus, a Christ of God, as it was written by the prophets. In the same way, Paul began his letter to the Romans. Paul introduced himself as a messenger (apostle) called to preach "the Gospel of God, which God promised beforehand by his prophets in Holy Scriptures" (Romans 1:2). Mark began by quoting the prophets Malachi and Isaiah, both of whom are quoted in Paul's letters. The New Testament began where the Old left off. Mark began his Gospel with the ending words of the prophet Malachi, the last book of the Old Testament.

As we shall see, Mark described the life of Jesus as the mirror image of the development of the Old Covenant, in the same way, Paul developed the significance of the bread and wine of the Lord's Supper (1 Corinthians 10:1–11). Mark and the other authors of the Gospel followed the lead of Paul. They fashioned the story of the life of Jesus to fulfill the predictions of the Old Testament about God's establishment of the New Covenant through the Christ of God.

Mark began his Gospel with the baptism of Jesus at the hands of John the Baptist in the river Jordan: "As he came out of the water, Jesus saw the heavens opening and the Spirit descending upon him like a dove (Mark 1:9–12). The spirit drove him into the wilderness. Jesus was in the wilderness for forty days. Satan tempted him. Angels ministered to him" (Mark 1:13).

Mark's description paralleled Paul's experience following his baptism in Damascus at the hand of the apostle of "the Way" named Ananias (Acts 9:10–20). Following his baptism, Paul, too, went into the wilderness for some period of time (Galatians 1:17). Both Jesus and Paul began preaching a Gospel. Jesus preached the Gospel of the kingdom of God while Paul preached the Gospel of God with Jesus as the Son of God (Romans 1:1; Acts 9:20). Mark correlated Paul's time in the wilderness as an experience of Jesus. Both of them fulfilled the role of the messenger of the covenant.

Luke and Matthew elaborated on the story of Jesus in the wilderness and described the temptation of Jesus as the tempting of God by the Israelites in the Exodus, which led to the establishment of the Mosaic Covenant. The first three Gospels are referred to the as the synoptic Gospels, because they copy one another in describing their experience of being a Christ of God.

In Luke, the first temptation about turning stone into bread correlated with the Exodus story of the bread from heaven called manna (Exodus 16:1–15; Luke 4:3). Luke's second temptation about the worship of God correlated with the Exodus story about the worship the golden calf (Exodus 32:1–7). Luke's third temptation about the proof that Jesus was the son of God correlated with the Exodus story about proving Jesus to be God's Son under the charge of angels (Exodus 17:1–7; Deuteronomy 6:16). Mathew edited Luke's account of the temptations and put them in the chronological order of the Exodus stories by exchanging Luke's second temptation with his third temptation.

The sojourns of Jesus and Paul in the wilderness led to their ministry as messengers of the covenant in the same way that the Israelites wandered in the wilderness for forty years and found the Ark of the Covenant's entry into the promised land. As we have already seen,

Paul connected these sojourns and wanderings with one another. At the same time, Paul connected the temptations of the Israelites during their wanderings in the wilderness with the temptations Christians experienced as a newborn Christ of God.

> I would not have you ignorant how all our fathers were under the cloud and all passed through the sea. All ate of the same spiritual meat [manna and quails] and all drank the same spiritual drink, for they drank of the spiritual Rock that followed them. That Rock was Christ. But with many of them God was not well pleased for they were over thrown in the wilderness. Now these things were *examples* so that we should not lust after evil things, as they lusted. Do not be idolaters, as were some of them. Do not let us commit fornication. Neither let us tempt Christ, as some of them also tempted. All these things happened unto them for examples. They were written for our admonition. Let those thinking they stand take heed lest they fall. No temptation has taken hold of you but such as is common to any human. God is faithful. He will not suffer you to be tempted above what you are able. With the temptation he will also make a way for you to escape. (1 Corinthians 10:1–14)

After the temptation story, Mark indicated that Jesus began his ministry when he learned Herod Antipas had imprisoned John the Baptist. Jesus proclaimed, "The time is fulfilled and the kingdom of God is at hand. Repent and believe the Gospel." Jesus's opening words reflect Paul's comments about the ministry of Christians:

> Any person who is in Christ is a new creature. All things are from God who has by Jesus, a Christ of God, given us the ministry of reconciliation. In Christ God was reconciling the world to Himself. Now we are ambassadors of Christ. (2 Corinthians 5:17–21)

Paul goes on to quote Isaiah:

In an acceptable time have I [God] heard you, and in a day of salvation have I helped you. I [God] will preserve you and give you as a covenant to the people. (Isaiah 49:8; 2 Corinthians 6:2)

Luke (4:14–21) indicated Jesus began his ministry with Isaiah's description of God's calling him to preach the Gospel:

The Spirit of the Lord is upon me, because He has anointed me to preach Gospel to the poor. He has sent me to heal the broken hearted, to preach deliverance to the captives, and recovering of sight to the blind, to set at liberty those who are bruised. They shall be called trees of righteousness, the planting of the Lord. Jesus went on to say: "This day is this scripture fulfilled in your ears." (Isaiah 61:1)

Again we find Paul making a similar comment. He wrote, "God has shined in our heart to give the light of the knowledge of the glory of God in the face of Jesus, a Christ of God (2 Corinthians 3:14–18; 4:6).

Mathew (4:12–17) wrote of the beginning of Jesus's preaching in this fashion:

When Jesus heard John the Baptist had been cast into prison, Jesus went from Nazareth to dwell in Capernaum, which is on the sea coast on the border of Zebulon and Nephthalim, so that the words spoken by Isaiah might be fulfilled: "The people of the land of Zabulon and Nephthalim who sat in darkness have seen a great light sprung up on the region and shadow of death." (Isaiah 9:1)

Isaiah goes on to say, "For unto us a child is born, unto us a son is given, and the government shall be on his shoulders. His name shall be called 'Wonderful, Counselor, The Mighty God, The Everlasting Father, The Prince of Peace.'" (Isaiah 9:6; 2 Corinthians 4:6)

Fulfillment

Fulfillment is a theme that runs throughout the New Testament. Paul wrote to the Romans, "Now the God of hope fill you with all joy and peace in believing, so that you may abound in hope, through the Holy Ghost. *You* are *full of goodness, filled with all* knowledge" (Romans 15:14).

The fundamental structure of the synoptic Gospels portrayed the life of Jesus as the fulfillment of the prophecies in the Old Testament. Each of Gospel authors wrote from their own experience enlightened by the insights of Paul.

Mark saw Jesus's ministry as the development of the kingdom of the Christ of God in keeping with Paul's comment, "God has delivered from the power of darkness and translated us into the kingdom of his beloved Son (Colossians 1:12–14). As Christians, we are in God's Kingdom here and now.

Luke saw Jesus's ministry as the fulfillment of Isaiah's preaching of Gospel to proclaim the acceptable year of the Lord God, which led to our being called trees of righteousness, the planting of the Lord showing forth the glory of the life of God (Isaiah 61:3). Paul wrote of our being planted trees of righteousness as servants of God who bring forth fruit of holiness (Romans 6:5, 23). Matthew's summation of Jesus's ministry as the fulfillment of Isaiah's prophecy—a child would be born who would bring light to those who sat in darkness—promised a similar declaration by Paul. Paul wrote of the Galatians as his children. He had suffered travail waiting until they were born again, and the Christ was then formed in them (Galatians 4:19).

John, like Matthew, set the stage for his Gospel in the theme of our being born again of water (purification) and the spirit of God (John 3:5). We have to be born of water and the Spirit. Paul's comment about the glory of God shining from our faces is the source for John's comment.

The New Imitates the Old

With his beginning, Mark described Jesus's ministry in the same way the Old Covenant was established when ark of the New Covenant came to the promised land. We have seen how Paul correlated the exodus with baptism and the Lord God's Supper. Mark likened Jesus's baptism to the Israelite passage through the Red Sea. Jesus's forty-day sojourn in the desert corresponded with the Israelites forty years of wandering in the wilderness, during which Moses developed the Mosaic Covenant of obedience to the law. The ritual of the Lord's Supper was based on eating manna as the body of the bread of Christ and drinking wine as though it was the life of the Christ of God (1 Corinthians 10:13–18, 21), and this ritual is similar to the one by which the Israelite committed themselves to obedience of Mosaic Covenant with their eating of the meat of the sacrifice and having some of the blood of the sacrifice sprinkled on them (Exodus 24:4–8).

Mark's account of the two feedings of multitudes in the wilderness was comparable to the two feedings in the Old Testament (Exodus 16:13; Numbers 11:31). Jesus's visitation to the synagogues of Israel was akin to the monthly visitation of the Ark of the Covenant taken by the Levites to the various tribes of Israel before the Ark was taken into Jerusalem by David. Mark described Jesus's entry into Jerusalem as similar to David's bringing the Ark of the Covenant into Jerusalem to establish a temple for the Ark (2 Samuel 6:1–19). The New Covenant began with Jesus's death on the cross in Jerusalem.

Mark's Gospel also included a number of incidents similar to both Jesus and Paul. Jesus demeaned Peter in front of others (Mark 8:32), Peter took exception to Jesus's telling them that his visit to Jerusalem would lead to Jesus's being put to death and would rise again on the third day. The incident is similar to Paul's confrontation with Peter (Galatians 2:11–14) when Paul accused Peter of refusing to eat with the uncircumcised in obedience to the rules of the Law. Jesus actually made that comment three times (Mark 8:31; 9:31 and 10:33). Other common experiences included that both were scourged by lashes (Mark 15:15; 2 Corinthians 1123). Both were shipwrecked and had to calm the distress of others (Mark 6:45–52; Matthew 14:22–33; Acts 27:2–44; 2 Corinthians 11:25). Both ministered along the shore of large bodies of water: Jesus at the Sea of Galilee and Paul around the Aegean Sea. Both were expelled from cities (Mark 5:14–17; Acts 14:1–7). Both were arrested under false pretenses, which ultimately led to their executions (Mark 15:1; Luke 23:1; Acts 21:27–33). Jesus was accused of calling himself the King of the Jews. Paul was accused of taking uncircumcised men into the temple, which led to his imprisonment in Caesarea and ultimately his death in Rome after Nero set the city afire. Both had come to Jerusalem to celebrate a holy day—Jesus at the Passover and Paul at Pentecost (Mark 14:12; Acts 20:16).

The Body of Christ

As we have already seen, Mark and Paul declared that the Gospel of God is based on the writings of the prophets. Now we find the Gospel of Jesus Christ to be based on the life of Paul. Paul also was a Christ. He was the one who understood the significance of the death and resurrection of the Christ in Jesus. But there was a predecessor essential to Paul's development of the Gospel of Jesus Christ. Paul's experience on the road to Damascus depended upon the preaching of John the Baptist. Without John, Paul would not have had his Damascus Road experience.

The four Gospel authors described the effect of John the Baptist not just in Paul's experience but also in the multitudes of converts from Judaism. Most of the followers of St. Paul were the Greek converts of the Gates who responded his message that everyone was the same before God. They came to dominate Christianity.

The other writers of the Gospels followed Mark's basic framework. Luke and Matthew copied Mark's Gospel, cutting it into small sections interspersed with their own insights. Luke opened his Gospel with the conception and birth of John the Baptist (Luke 1:11–25). He followed with the virgin birth of Jesus and with the baptism of John the Baptist as the role of Elijah (Luke 4–12), whom Malachi said would come before the day of the Lord when God would appear in the "temple/body" of the messenger of the covenant (Malachi 3:1–3). Luke's theme was the establishment of the kingdom of God through the New Covenant (Luke 22:16).

Matthew opened his Gospel with the genealogy of Jesus, tracing his birth through Abraham to Adam, and our heritage as Christians to the promises God made to Abraham (Matthew 1:1-17). Matthew described the virgin birth of Jesus, noting his reference, "This was done [written] to fulfill what was spoken by the prophet Isaiah: 'A virgin shall be with child and shall bring forth a son'" (Matthew 1:22f; Isaiah 7:14). Isaiah and Jeremiah identified the virgin as "the virgin daughter of Israel" (Isaiah 23:12; 27:22; Jeremiah 14:17; 18:13; 31:4; Lamentations 1:15; 2:13; Amos 5:2). Isaiah wrote (62:5), "As a young man marries a virgin and rejoices over the bride, so shall God rejoice over you." Hosea (2:18) made a similar prophecy in connection with his remarks about those who were not God's people becoming his people: "In that day I will make a covenant with them ... I will betroth [them] unto me forever in righteousness and judgment ... [in] loving kindness and mercies and in faithfulness and they shall know the Lord [God]." Paul made the same observation: *"You [are to be] married to him [Jesus, the Christ of God] who is raised from the dead that we might bring forth fruit [the Christ of God] unto God" (Romans 7:4).* "I have *espoused you to one husband, that I may present you as a chaste virgin to the Christ of God"* (2 Corinthians 11:2). The Apostles' Creed indicates that the Christ of God was "conceived by the Holy Spirit and born of the Virgin Mary" (Apostle's Creed, *The Book of Common Prayer, printed* for The Episcopal Church; Kingsbury Press, Kingsbury, Tennessee 1977, 53). The Virgin Mary represented the people of Israel. The Virgin birth is about the birth of Christ in us (Galatians 4:19).

Paul's comment that we are to be married to Christ in order to bring forth fruit onto God (Romans 7:4) reflects Isaiah's prophecy:

> O barren who did not bear children, your maker is your husband, your redeemer, the Holy One of Israel. The Lord [God] has called you as a woman forsaken and grieved in spirit and a wife of youth. I [God] will have everlasting kindness. My covenant of peace shall not be taken from you. Your children shall be taught of the Lord [God]. This is the heritage of the servants of the Lord and their righteousness is of me. (Isaiah 54:1–17)

God is both our father as our creator and our husband whose seed is born as Christ in us when we are born of His spirit by leading us in His life each day. Luke's story of the virgin birth declares the fulfillment of the prophecy from the experience of his own life. We, too, are born again just as Christ was born in Mary, and as Christ was born in Jesus. Jesus was not Christ until his baptism, when the Holy Spirit descended upon him.

To be born in the Christ of God is to be born again to eternal life. Eternal life is the theme of John's Gospel. He opened his Gospel by tracing its beginning to the creation of the universe by the word of God, noting, "All things were made by him [God] and without him was not anything brought into being" (John 1:3).

John's opening words echo Paul's statement: "To us there is but one God, the Father, of whom are all things, and we in Him and one Lord Jesus, the Christ of God, by whom are all things, and we by Him" (1 Corinthians 8:6; Colossians 1:16; Psalm 33:6.). John went on to say, "In Him was life and the life was the light of men. The light shined in the darkness, and the darkness did not comprehend it" (John 1:1–5). These words echo Paul's writings: "You were sometimes darkness, but now are you light in the Lord; walk as children of light" (Ephesians 5:8).

John continued, "He came into his own [Israelites] and his own did not receive Him. To those who received Him he gave power [the Holy Spirit] to become the sons of God, who were … born of God. The word was made flesh and dwelt in us, and we beheld His glory, as of an [offspring] only begotten of the Father, full of grace and truth" (John 1:12–15). In his letter to the Romans, Paul writes, "All who are led by the spirit of God … are the children of God … whereby we cry Abba, Father" (Romans 8:14–16).

John's first miracle of Jesus was set on the third day at a wedding in Cana of Galilee, when Jesus turned the water into wine (John 2:1–11). The third day signified the era of the resurrection had started, reflecting Paul's revelation about the resurrection's inauguration on the third day and his espousal of the Corinthians to the Christ of God (2 Corinthians 11:2). In John's Gospel, Jesus made his first visit to Jerusalem earlier than in the other Gospels, but he also visited at the time of Passover, cleansing of the temple, signifying the resurrection began with forgiveness of our ungodliness as a chaste virgin (John 2:13–25).

The next event in John's Gospel was the conversation of the Rabbi, Nicodemus, "who came to him by night," about the need to be born. Jesus never answered Nicodemus's question: "How can a man be born again. Can he enter again into his mother's womb?" (John 3:1–8). Jesus simply restated his comment about being born again and said, "Except a man be born of water and the Spirit, he cannot enter into the kingdom of God;" again a reflection of Paul's statement to the Galatians about being in travail until the Christ of God was born in them (Galatians 4:19). In the first three chapters, John summarized the other Gospels, and from there on, he continued to quote them haphazardly. Throughout his Gospel, however, John's chapters reflected the writings of St. Paul more than the other three.

In John's fifth chapter, Jesus spoke as though he were Paul. Jesus was accused of saying he was equal with God (John 5:18) just as Paul declared the same equality in his letter to the Philippians (Philippians 2:6). Jesus went on to say, "As the Father gives life so does the Son (John 5:21)," which was similar to Paul's comment, "We were reconciled to God by [the Christ of God's] death, we shall be saved by His life" (Romans 5:10).

John the Baptist Sets the Stage

The ministry of John the Baptist marked the beginning of all the Gospels.

The Baptist's preaching led Jesus to become the suffering servant of Isaiah's prophecy (Isaiah 52:13; 53:1–8). The clue to the significance of John's endeavors was the description of his clothing and diet, which matched that of the prophet Elijah. Mark's opening words direct us to the Books of Malachi and Isaiah to understand the role John played. He wrote the following:

> *The beginning* of the Gospel of Jesus, the Christ of God, the Son of God; as it is written in the prophets, "Behold, I send my messenger before your face to prepare your way before you. (Mark 1; Malachi 4:5)

> The voice of one crying in the wilderness, "Prepare you the way of the Lord, make his paths straight." (Mark 1:3; Isaiah 40:3)

> John baptized in the wilderness, preaching the baptism of repentance for the remission of sins. *John was clothed with camel's hair about his loins, and did eat locusts and wild honey.* (Mark 1:4–6; Malachi 4:5)

57

Mark's introduction indicated the Gospel of Jesus, the Christ of God, began before Jesus was born. Mark's comments pointed to the prophets for understanding the Gospel message. Malachi's prophecy is the last book of the Old Testament. The New Testament began where the Old ended. Malachi indicated there would be two messengers: One would be the messenger who prepared the way for God to come to His temple. Another messenger who would be a different person, one who would be both the temple of God and the messenger of the covenant.

> Behold, I will send my messenger [first messenger], and he shall prepare the way before me; and the Lord whom you seek shall suddenly come to His temple, even the messenger of the covenant, in whom you delight [second messenger]. (Malachi 3:1)

The last words of the Hebrew Bible indicated Elijah would be the second messenger. God would send a messenger to call the people to repentance before God came to His temple.

> Behold, I will send you Elijah the prophet before the coming of the great and dreadful day of the Lord God's coming to the temple [the body of the Christ of God]; and he [Elijah] shall turn the hearts of the fathers to the children and hearts of the children to their fathers [repentance], lest I [God] come and smite the land with a curse. (Malachi 4:5)

Malachi's prophecy was the foundation of Paul's understanding of the Gospel of God: "You are the temple of God and the Spirit of dwells in you" (1 Corinthians 3:16).

Mark cast John in the role of Elijah [the first messenger] when he wrote *that John wore camel's hair and a leather girdle around his loins and ate locusts and wild honey.* The Talmud made the comment about Elijah's diet of locusts and honey. The Bible identified Elijah as a hairy man with a girdle around his loins in the story about King Ahaziah's sending messengers to inquire of a foreign God. On their way, the messengers met a man they didn't recognize who made them turn back, because God told him that Ahaziah would surely die. Ahaziah asked the messengers who the man was, and "they answered, 'He was a hairy man with a girdle of leather about his loin. And Ahaziah said, 'It is Elijah, the Tishbite'" (2 Kings 1:2–8).

The other Gospels followed Mark's lead. All of them put John's baptism of Jesus as a precursor to the beginning of Jesus's ministry. Luke opened his Gospel with the miraculous birth of John the Baptist, whom Luke described as a cousin of Jesus. John would "be called the prophet of the Highest, for he would go before the face of the Lord to prepare his ways" (Luke 1:76). Matthew referred to the kingdom as the kingdom of heaven as opposed to Mark and Luke's reference to the kingdom as the kingdom of God. John the Baptist was reluctant to baptize Jesus, saying, "I have need to be baptized by you" (Mathew 3:13f). John gave witness that he saw the spirit of God descending on Jesus at his baptism. Paul wrote, "The kingdom of God is righteousness, peace, and joy in the Holy Spirit as servants of Christ" (Romans 14:17).

John the Baptist's message of a baptism of repentance for the forgiveness of sins found favor in the synagogues around the Mediterranean. It appealed to both Jewish and to Gentile converts to Judaism. Baptismal commitment to repentance for forgiveness of transgression eased the guilt for failing to make the temple sacrifices required by the law. The Gentile converts were known as proselytes of righteousness or proselytes of the gates, the latter also being referred as "God fearers" or as "those who feared God." The proselytes of righteousness measured righteousness by obedience to the law. They were accepted as loyal Jews. The proselytes of the gates did not follow all the laws. They were attracted to the idea of one God and to the worship of Judaism. They were allowed to worship with the Jews, but they could not eat with them or enter their homes. Their feeling about their position in Judaism was spelled out in the words of Isaiah: "Though Abraham be ignorant of us and Israel does not acknowledge us; thou art our father, and redeemer" (Isaiah 63:16). John's message prepared the way for Paul's message.

Paul's Disputation with John the Baptist

Paul found himself between a rock and a hard place with regard to John the Baptist. On the one hand, John had drawn a large following to his message based on obedience to the law and the commandments. On the other hand, the proselytes of the gates were attracted to the preaching of Paul. Paul regarded obedience to the laws of Judaism as death to the life of God. The gift of the Holy Ghost was life. Paul wrote the following:

> As you have received the Christ of God, Jesus, the Lord, so walk in him. For in Jesus' flesh dwells all the fullness of the Godhead. You are fulfilled in him … putting off the body of the transgressions of the flesh. Buried with [Jesus] you are risen from the dead [the 'they' world]. Being dead [to the 'they' world], God has made you alive, blotting out the handwriting [the written law] of ordinances that was against us, and nailing it to a tree. If you are dead to the rudiments of the world, why are you subject to ordinances, commandments, and doctrines of men? (Colossians 2:6–23)

Paul's message had a mixed reception from the followers of John the Baptist. The Jews and the proselytes of righteousness accused him of blasphemy. The converts of the gates took heart, because his message put everyone on the same level:

> You are all the children of God by the faith (which is in you as it is) in Jesus, a Christ of God. There is neither Jew nor Greek. There is neither bond nor free. There is neither male nor female, circumcision nor uncircumcision, for you are all one in the Christ of God. If you belong to the Christ of God, then you are Abraham's seed and heirs according to the promise. God will not suffer you to be tempted above what you may be able to bear. (Galatians 3:26–29; Colossians 3:11)

Paul began his preaching about AD 40. John the Baptist was beheaded around AD 26. The message attributed to John the Baptist in Mark's Gospel is anachronistic. Paul was the first to preach the Gospel about the Holy Spirit fifteen years after John's death. Paul was writing of the Christ of God in Jesus, which was risen in those who died to the life of the iconoclastic 'they' world to live the life of God. An incident involving the preaching of a Jew named Apollos indicated the followers of "the Way" had never heard about the Holy Ghost until the preaching of Paul.

Apollos was a Jew, born in Alexandria. He was an eloquent man, well-versed in the scriptures. He was instructed in "the Way" of the Lord. He came to Ephesus, where he taught about "the Way," knowing only the baptism of John. Aquila and Priscilla, with whom Paul had lived in Corinth, heard Apollos speak. They searched him out to explain to him the way of the Christ of God, which Apollos embraced. Apollos then went to Corinth with a letter of introduction from Aquila and Priscilla. There, Apollos convinced many of the Jews that Jesus was a Christ of God.

When Paul returned from his second missionary journey, he was told about Apollos. He inquired about certain followers of "the Way" on the outskirts of Ephesus, asking if they had received the Holy Ghost. They told him they had not so much as heard of the Holy Ghost when they were baptized with John's baptism, whereupon they were baptized in the name of the Lord Jesus (Acts 18:24–19:5).

Sometime later, this incident led Paul to write about it in his first letter to the Corinthians. Paul had learned of dissension within the church. The members bragged about who baptized whom, whether it was Peter or Apollos or Paul. Paul asked, "Is Christ divided? Was Paul crucified for you? Were you baptized in the name of Paul?" (1 Corinthians 1:10–13). He goes on to write, "One says, 'I am of Paul,' and another, 'I am of Apollos.' Are not you then carnal [of the flesh of the self-exalted 'they' world]? Who, then, is Paul, and who is Apollos, but ministers by whom you believed? I have planted; Apollos watered, but God gives the increase" (1 Corinthians 3:4–7).

The people following John the Baptist came to be known as "the People of the Way." Without the knowledge of the Holy Spirit, John's preaching led them to measure righteousness by obedience to the law. Paul preached just the opposite. Those who lived by the law would die by the law.

Chapter Five

The Grace of God

Faith and the Law

Though Paul was at odds with John's message of obedience to the law, he recognized the success of John the Baptist's message. Without speaking of "the People of the Way," Paul recognized them as part of the remnant God promised to Elijah and Malachi in prophecy. In his letter to the Romans, Paul quoted Elijah's intercession to God about his people "whom He would not forsake if they followed the good and right way of fearing [reverencing] the Lord and serving Him in truth with all their heart" (1 Samuel 12:21–24). Paul quoted Elijah's intercession and elaborated on how God answered through Paul's message in this fashion:

> Elijah made intercession to God against Israel saying, "They have killed thy prophets and dug down God's altars. I am alone, and they seek my life." God replied to Elijah, "I have reserved to myself seven thousand men, who have not bent the to the image of Baal." (1 Kings 19:10, 18; Romans 11:3)

Paul then gave the following comment:

Even so at the present time there is also a remnant according to [God's] election of grace [gift]. If it is by grace, it is not of works. I speak to you Gentiles, inasmuch as I am the apostle to the Gentiles, if by any means, I may provoke you to emulate them [the Jewish remnant], which are of my flesh, and might save some of them. What shall their reception be, other than life from the dead [resurrection]?" (Romans 11:1–15)

Paul's commentary ran hand in glove with Malachi's prophecy, which ended with Elijah's return to warn the people. Malachi wrote the following (3:13–4:6):

You have been strongly against me, says the Lord. Yet you say, "What have we spoken against you?" You have said, "It is meaningless to serve the God"; and "what value is there in keeping His ordinances?" You call the proud happy. Those who work wickedness are exalted.

Those who feared [revered] the Lord spoke to one another and the Lord hearkened and heard it. A book of remembrance was written for them [the remnant] who feared the Lord and respected His name. They shall be mine in that day when I make up my [elect]. I will spare them as a man [favors] his own son who serves him.

Behold, the day is coming, which shall burn as an oven. All the proud and those who do wickedly shall be stubble. But unto you who fear [revere] my name shall the Sun arise [the light of understanding]. You shall go forth and grow as calves set free from the stall.

Remember the law of Moses, which I commanded to him for all Israel with the statutes and judgments. Behold, *I will send you Elijah before the coming of the Lord and he shall turn the heart of the children to the fathers, and the heart of the fathers to the children, lest I come and smite the land with a curse.*

From my perspective, Paul saw himself as one of Elijah's seven thousand Jewish remnants after his Damascus experience. Furthermore, when Paul proclaimed himself to be the apostle to Gentiles, he put himself in the role of Elijah, as described in Malachi, preparing the way for God to appear suddenly in His temple. Paul was not a messenger of the law. The messenger of the law was John the Baptist. Paul was the messenger of the faith revealed in Jesus, a Christ of God: He wrote of his own experience spending his life in the study of holy scripture and finding the law to be his death to the life of God:

> For I through the law am dead to the law, so that I might live unto God. I am crucified with the Christ of God; nevertheless I live. Yet it is not I [who lives]. It is the Christ of God who lives in me; and the life, which I now live, *I live by the faith of the Son of God, who gave himself for me.... If righteousness comes by the law, then the Christ of God died in vain.* The Christ of God has redeemed us from the curse of the law, being made a curse for us, as it is written, "Cursed is everyone hanged on a tree." (Galatians 2:19-21; 3:13; Deuteronomy 21:23)

> Before faith came, we were kept under the law, shut up unto the faith, which afterwards He revealed. The law was our schoolmaster to bring us to Christ that we might be justified (made righteous) by faith. But after faith is come, we are no longer under a schoolmaster. You, who have been baptized into the Christ of God, have put on the Christ of God. (Galatians 3:24–27)

> When we were children, we were in bondage under the elements of world (into which we were born). When the fullness of time was come, God sent forth his Son, made of a woman, made under the law, to redeem them that were under the law, so that we might receive the adoption of sons. God has sent forth the Spirit of His

Son into your hearts, whereby we cry, "Abba, father."
You are no more a servant, but a Son. If a son, then
we are an heir of God through the Christ of God.
(Galatians 4:3–2, 7)

In his letter to the Romans, Paul identified himself as Malachi's
"temple of God, the messenger of the covenant," and also as Elijah,
"Malachi's messenger sent to prepare the way before God": "Paul a
servant as of Jesus, the Christ of God, called to be an apostle, separated
unto the Gospel of God" (Romans 1:1).

Anyone living the life of God is the temple where God lives. At the
same time, the emotion of His life stirs up the seed in those around
them preparing the way for them to follow. Whether or not they preach
the message, the choice of being is made on a level playing ground.
Although the 'they' world may show itself first as a choice of being, the
life of God is just as powerful. In truth, I have read stories where people
of the 'they' world risked their lives to help someone in deep distress. If
the response comes from a heartfelt sympathy for the person then the
action is a response to the call of God to be as He is. You would then be
a Christ of God. If you do something because "it is the Christian thing
to do," you would be doing it for yourself and not for the well-being
of the other person. You just blew yourself out of the water. Choosing
the high road is choosing because you see someone in distress in one
way or another and not because you want to earn brownie points with
God. You become a servant of God for as long as you follow the road
of righteousness now open to you.

The word translated as "servant" may also be translated as "slave."
The word basically refers to a "bondman." But there are two types of
bondmen. It depends on whether the bondman comes into bondage
willingly or unwillingly. The word "servant" is used when the bondman
chooses bondage of his own accord for which he receives pay for a
specific time. The word "slave" is used when the bondman is sold
unwillingly into bondage. (Leviticus 25: 39-55). Paul chose to be a
servant willingly, dying to life under the law. Instead of doing their
work willingly for payment of services, Paul and Jesus chose to become
servants of God for nothing (Philippians 2:5-8)

An apostle is a servant sent to carry a message. Paul's message is the
life of God radiating from the face of the apostle. The Nicene Creed

indicates that all Christians are also the messengers as Christians with the statement in the Nicene Creed, born of God, as members of "the holy, universal, and *apostolic* [messenger] church."

The Cross of Salvation

Previous discussion (see section titled "John the Baptist Set the Stage") connected John the Baptist with the role of the first messenger mentioned in Malachi's prophecy. Additional consideration reveals how Malachi's prophecy also lead to Isaiah's prophecy about the preparation of "the Way" for God to appear in His temple, which in turn lead to our salvation by the cross. Mark's opening words described Jesus as the temple in whom God would appear as the messenger of Isaiah's New Covenant. He changes the pronoun "me," which referred to God, to "you," whoever was the reader of the Gospel of Mark.

> I [God] send my messenger before your face, who shall prepare the way before you. The voice of one crying in the wilderness, "Prepare you the way of the Lord [God] make his paths straight." (Mark 1:2)

Malachi indicated the messenger would prepare the way for God to come to his temple, which would be the messenger of the covenant. However, Malachi's covenant was not the covenant of Mark. Malachi's covenant was the law of Moses with its statutes and judgments. Malachi complained about the corrupt sacrifices and the unpaid tithes required by the law (Malachi 1:7f; 3:8). We have just seen how Paul considered the law and ordinances of Moses as a curse. On the other hand, the covenant of Mark was Isaiah's covenant of the spirit:

> Behold, my servant upon whom I have put my spirit. The Lord called him in righteousness and *gave him as a covenant for the people to open the eyes of the blind and to bring forth the prisoner s who sit in darkness.* (Isaiah 42:1–7)

Jesus became a Christ of God at his baptism when the spirit of God descended on him like a dove. Like Paul, Jesus was raised from the dead, who were the Jews seeking righteousness by the Old Covenant. As the messenger of the new covenant, Jesus, a Christ of God, prepared the way for the Holy Spirit for those who were drawn to the presence of God emanating from the face of Jesus. Jesus, a Christ of God, prepared the way for God to appear in the temple of those with ears to hear and eyes to see the presence of God as Isaiah wrote:

> God will come to save [bring salvation to] you. Then the eyes of the blind shall be opened, and the ears of the deaf unstopped. The lame man shall leap like a hart and the tongue of the dumb shall sing. A highway will be there, and away. It will be called The Way of Holiness. The unclean shall not pass over it. (Isaiah 35:4–8)

Paul echoed Isaiah's words in his letter to the Corinthians in which he wrote, "The cross is foolishness to them who perish, but unto us who are saved [healed] it is the power of God" (1 Corinthians 1:18). Mark cast the cross as the key to salvation with Jesus's answer about living eternal life: "Take up your cross and follow me" (Mark 10:17–21). The empty cross signifies our dying to the 'they' world to live the life of God. Paul made this clear when wrote that the glory of salvation lay in the cross of Jesus, by whom the world was crucified unto him and him unto the world (Galatians 6:14). Salvation signified the healing in being anointed with salve of the life of God.

An essential aspect of Paul's understanding of the Gospel of God was the presence of God since the beginning of our creation when God inspirited Himself into man and man became a living soul. Malachi's statement about God suddenly coming to His temple should be understood as His appearance. God was already present in mankind as a seed in a dormant state. We become the temple of God when we choose the care-fulness road of God's life. It was then that God dwells in us, and we became a Christ of God, the messengers of the covenant (1 Corinthians 3:16).

Everyone who lets go of the low road of *carelessness* in order to choose the high road of the life of *carefulness* becomes a Christ of God. Every human alive today can be a Christ of God, just as Jesus, Paul, and the authors of the four Gospels were in their time. Jesus takes precedence as the first human to reveal the opportunity to be a Christ of God by living the life of God even in the face of death.

The opportunity has always been present in all mankind since the beginning of creation. Jesus was human and divine in every way. As we have already seen, Paul and Mark made Jesus's humanity clear when he wrote of the lineage of Jesus and his baptism:

> Jesus was born of the sperm of David according to the flesh. And was declared to be *a* Son God, with power according to the spirit of holiness by resurrection of the dead. (Romans 1:3)

> And coming up out of the water he saw the heavens open and the Spirit descending upon him like a dove. There was a voice from heaven, saying, "You are my beloved Son in whom I am well pleased." Immediately the spirit drove him into the wilderness. He was there in the wilderness forty days, tempted of Satan and with the wild beasts [while] angels ministered to his [needs]. (Mark 1:9–13)

The New Testament Exodus

The themes, which lay behind the structure of Mark's Gospel, began with Jesus's baptism. Jesus did not have the Holy Spirit prior to his baptism. He was in bondage under the law just as the Jews were in bondage under the Egyptians. Jesus, living under the elements of his world of obedience to the law, was dead to the life of God. *According to Mark, at his baptism, Jesus was raised from the dead life of alienation from the life of God and then joined his flesh with the self of God to become a Christ of God.* As he came out of the water, he saw the heavens open; the spirit like a dove descended on him and immediately led him into the wilderness. He stayed in the wilderness forty days and was tempted of Satan at every turn. Angels ministered to his needs for food and water. The forty days he spent in the wilderness reflected the forty years the Jews spent in the wilderness. Time and time again, the Jews put

God to the test about His care for them. Mark's description of Jesus's baptism paralleled Paul's comments about the wilderness experience of the Jews:

Paul went on to write:

Our fathers were under the cloud, and all passed through the sea. All were *baptized unto Moses in the cloud and in the sea*. All ate the same spiritual food. All drank of the same spiritual drink, for they drank of the Rock that followed them. That rock was the Christ of God. (1 Corinthians 10:1–4)

Mark next described an indefinite hiatus after Jesus's sojourn in the wilderness. Jesus waited until John the Baptist was put in prison before he came into Galilee and preached the Gospel of the kingdom of God (Mark 1:14). Jesus spent most of his time in the wilderness because of the crowds He attracted in the cities. He healed many people just by touching them. Mark ended many healings with Jesus's comments that a person being "made whole by their faith" and should "sin no more."

The miracles of wholeness signified a fulfillment of the destiny to which we are called. They were miracles of purification and cleanliness. Wholeness means being at one with ourselves and with God. We cease being led by the spirit of the selfless 'they' world as we choose to be led by the Holy Spirit. We become the offspring of God, Christs of God.

Paul similarly wrote of what it meant to belong to God:

I beseech you, brethren, to present yourselves as living sacrifices, holy and acceptable to God in the service of His word [the service of our expressing ourselves as the self of God]. Be not confirmed to this world but be transformed by the renewing of your mind and *prove what is the good and acceptable will of God*. (Romans 12f)

Let love be without dissimilation. Abhor what is evil. Cleave to what is good. Be kindly affectionate to one another with brotherly love, in honor preferring one another, not slothful in spirit, serving the Lord, rejoicing in hope, continuing instant in prayer. Bless those who persecute you and curse them not. Rejoice with those who rejoice and weep with those who weep. Be of the same mind to one another. Mind not high things, but condescend to men of low estate. Be not wise in your conceits. Recompense to no one evil for evil. Provide things honest in the sight of all. Avenge not your selves, for it is written, 'vengeance is mine; I will repay,' says the Lord. If your enemy is hungry, feed him; if he thirsts, give him drink: for in doing so you shall heap coals of fire on his head. Be not overcome by evil, but overcome evil with good. (Romans 12:9–20; Proverbs 25:21)

As already noted, Paul elaborated on our becoming a Christ of God when he wrote the following:

> Every human's work shall be made manifest; it shall be revealed by fire. You are Christ's [of Christ], and Christ is God's [of God]. (1 Corinthians 3:13, 23)

Mark reflected Paul's comment about our being a Christ of God when he described the time Jesus took a child in his arms and said, "Whosoever shall receive one such child in my name, receives not me but Him who sent me" (Mark 9:37; Ephesians5:1f).

Matthew and Luke echoed Paul's words, attributing them to Jesus, a Christ of God. Matthew wrote, "Love your enemies, bless them that curse you, do good to them that hate you and pray for these who despitefully use you. That you may be the children of your Father in heaven" (Mathew 5: 43).

Mathew followed Luke's rendition of the Lord's Prayer, changing it to the version we know today. In my mind, this prayer is based on Paul's understanding of the Gospel of God, which is noted in italics and parentheses below: (Matthew 6:9; Luke 11:2).

> Our Father (*all who are led by the Spirit of God are the offspring of God...whereby we cry 'Abba, Father'* [Romans 8:14f]), who art in heaven, (*we have a building of God, a house not made with hands, eternal in the heavens. You are the temple of the living God. I will dwell in you* (2 Corinthians 5:1, 6:16]) hallowed be thy name, (*I have raised you [Moses] up so that my name be declared throughout all nations. Tell them my name is Yahweh,*

'*The Being*' (Romans 9:17; 14:11; Septuagint: Exodus 3:14), thy kingdom come (*The kingdom of God ... is righteousness and peace and joy in the Holy Ghost. Now is the accepted time; now is the day of salvation* [Romans 14:17; 2 Corinthians 6:2]), thy will be done (*Be transformed by the renewing of your mind so that you prove what is the good and acceptable will of God* [Romans 12:2]); give us this day our daily bread (*The bread which you break, is it not the communion of the body of Christ...which is broken for you in remembrance of me?* [1 Corinthians 10:16; 11:24]) forgive us our sins as we forgive those who sin against us; (*Be not overcome by evil, but overcome evil with good. Whoever's sins you remit, they are remitted; whoever's sins you retain, they are retained. If you forgive not men their trespasses, neither will God forgive your trespasses* [Romans 12:20f; John 20:23; Matthew 6:15]); Lead us not into temptation, but deliver us from evil (Avenge not yourselves, but rather put away wrath. Vengeance is mine; I will repay, says the Lord [Romans 12:19]); *For thine is the kingdom and the power and the glory; for ever* (The unrighteous shall not inherit the kingdom of God ... We preach Christ crucified, the power of God ... God has shined in our hearts, to give the light of the knowledge of the glory of God in the face of Jesus, a Christ of God. [1 Corinthians 1:23, 6:9; 2 Corinthians 4:6])

The Resurrection and the Third Day

The appearance of Jesus three days after his crucifixion rests at the heart of the four Gospels, yet the description of his resurrection appearances differ from one another and from Paul's epistles. There were no appearances in Mark at all. Mark's Verses 16:9-20 were not part of his original Gospel. Luke described the appearances as taking place on the road to Emmaus and in Jerusalem. Matthew placed the appearances on a mountain near Galilee. John wrote of Jesus's appearances in Jerusalem and Sea of Galilee. Paul wrote of Jesus's rising again from the dead on the third day like the scriptures describe. Paul indicated that Jesus appeared first to Peter and then to the twelve disciples, followed by five hundred at once, James, all the apostles, and finally to Paul himself as "one born out of time" (1 Corinthians 15:3–9).

Paul also pictured his Damascus experience as visions and revelations of the Lord when he found himself caught up into the third heaven: "Whether in the body or out of the body, I could not tell" (2 Corinthians 12:2). Paul also wrote of his experience as the time when God revealed the Son in him (Galatians 1:16). The appearances of a Christ of God were envisioned in the minds of Luke, Matthew, and John. They saw themselves suffering the pangs of childbirth as they died to the life alienated from God to be born again as an offspring of God. Their travail was like the pains of the crucifixion of Jesus. (Galatians 4:19)

The Christ of God dwelt in each of the New Testament authors. They were all messengers of the New Covenant. The authors of the New Testament wrote from their own experience of dying to the life of this world to live the life of the Christ of God. As they read the scriptures and Paul's letters, the Gospel authors discovered something worthwhile to understanding the God's gift of the Holy Spirit. Paul based the life of God on our being led by the spirit of God. Mark and Luke emphasized membership in the kingdom of God. Matthew wrote of it as membership in the kingdom of heaven. John described living the life of God as eternal life.

The scriptural source of the third-day resurrection, referred to by Paul, is found in the book of Hosea:

> I [God] will be unto Ephraim as a lion, and as a young lion to the house of Judah. I will tear [them into pieces] and go away. I will go and return to my place, till they acknowledge their offence and seek my face. Come, let us turn to the Lord; for he has torn, and he will heal us; he has smitten and he will bind us up. *After two days he will revive [heal] us he will raise us up, and we shall live in his sight. Then shall we know the Lord. He shall come to us as the morning [sunrise].* (Hosea 5:14–6:1)

According to Hosea, God's reviving us from death referred to our becoming a Christ of God. Hosea's reference to our living in His sight as knowing God connects the resurrection with our being born again even in adulthood. The Hebrew word here translated as "know" is the word used when Adam and Eve joined together as one flesh of husband and wife to give birth to their children (Genesis 4:1). Isaiah wrote of the resurrection as the birth of a child: "For unto us a child is born, unto us a son is given; and the government [the kingdom of God] will be on his shoulders (Isaiah 9:6). Isaiah later wrote:

> We are as fainthearted people thirsting in Zion. The Lord of hosts shall make a feast for all nations [who] shall drink gladness. They shall anoint [christen] themselves with ointment. Death has prevailed and swallowed men up, but again the Lord God has taken away every tear from their face. In that day they shall say, "Behold, our God in whom we have trusted, shall save us. We will rejoice in our salvation." In affliction, Lord, have I remembered you ... Your chastening was to us with small affliction ... As a woman in travail draws nigh to be delivered and cries out in her pain so have we been. We have conceived and have been in pain and *have brought forth the breath [spirit] of your salvation. The dead shall arise.* (Septuagint, Isaiah 25:4–9; 26:10–19)

Purification and Fore-giveness

Paul reflected Isaiah's prophecies in his epistles to the Galatians and the Corinthians: "I [Paul] have espoused you to one husband in order to present you to Christ as a chaste virgin. I travail in birth again until Christ be formed in you" (2 Corinthians 11:2; Galatians 4:19). Hosea's prophecy also described the resurrection of Christ as a healing in his epistles. Paul referred to resurrection to as a purification when he wrote the following:

> You are washed. You are sanctified. You are justified [made righteous] in the name of the Lord, Jesus, a

Christ of God, and by the spirit of our God. God has raised up the Lord [Jesus] and He [God] will also raise us up by His [God's] own power." Don't you know your bodies are the members of the body of Christ in you? Don't you know your body is the temple of the Holy Spirit, which God put in you? Your body is not your own. (1 Corinthians 6:11–17)

We are laborers together with God. You are God's husbandry [cultivation]. You are God's building. Don't you know you are the temple of God, and the Spirit of God dwells in you? You are Christ's and Christ is of God *[God's]*. (1 Corinthians 3:9, 16, 23)

Throughout the Old Testament, whatever went wrong—every sickness, every death, every drought—was considered to be the vengeance of God for failure to abide by Mosaic Covenant (Deuteronomy 32:35–43). On the other hand, Paul founded his preaching on God's mercy, not vengeance. Paul's perspective indicated those who sought righteousness through the law were deaf and blind to God's grace of redemption by faith in Jesus, a Christ of God. God's care for our well-being is not based on the law. It is based on dying to the corruptive 'they' world of obedience to the law. The law was ineffective as a means of righteousness. God was not vengeful. His relationship with us is forgiveness. He radiates forgiveness, mercy, kindness, and concern for the well-being of everyone and everything

On the careless road, the first choices will be animalistic: flee, fight, or freeze. Our emotional state will be in the range of anger, frustration, jealousy, one-upmanship, etc. Choices on the carefulness road will require patience, because they will always come second even when we are on the road of righteousness. Paul wrote that we should think on whatever things are true, honest, righteous, pure, lovely, and of good report (Philippians 4:8). Blessed are they whose iniquities are forgiven and in whom there is no guile (Psalm 32:1; Romans 4:7).

Forgiveness, like the tango, takes two. We have to accept the gift of the life of God. We have to be purified. We have to die to the life we have led. It isn't easy to tear ourselves away from our pasts. For one thing, we don't like to face our failure to fulfill our destiny as the offspring of God. For another, we will be like newborn children without the blemish of the world into which we were born from the womb. As newborn offspring, we have to learn what it means to be a Christ of God.

Paul had to learn it. That is why he went to Arabia after he was baptized. The universe is in constant change. We are always facing new situations. This is the essence of what it means to be in control of our being. Our world keeps changing, and we have to change with it. Of course, we will make mistakes. Paul acknowledged this when he wrote, "I die daily" (1 Corinthians 15:31).

The Lord's Prayer anticipates our failure to be an offspring of God. We will trespass off the high road of carefulness to find ourselves trespassing on the low road of carelessness. Look back on when you had to make an apology. Did you add a "but" afterward to put the blame on your parents or your teachers or the church or the government?

Christianity refers to purification as chastening while the 'they' world sees it as punishment. We are the only living things who have to choose our futures. We can either live in the world as a Christ of God in newness of life, or we can choose to be of the world of the past, dead to the life of the Christ of God. We can take a lead from Isaiah's prophesies: "This is the covenant with them, says the Lord, my spirit which is upon you and my words which I have put in your mouth. I shall create a new heaven and a new earth" (Isaiah 59:21; 65:17). Paul wrote the following as well:

> God has made us able ministers of the new covenant; not of the letter of the law [the covenant of the past], but of the Spirit [the covenant of our being as God is]; for the letter kills but the Spirit gives life … If any person be a Christ of God, that person is a new creature; old things have passed away, all thing are become new. Just as the Christ of God [in Jesus] was raised from the dead by the glory of the Father, so we also should walk in newness of life. Let us put on the armor of Light [understanding] [by raising us also]. Let us walk honestly. *Let us put on the Lord, Jesus, a Christ of God.* (*2 Corinthians 3:5; 5:17; Romans 6:4; 13:13*)

75

The resurrection of the Christ of God in Jesus takes place in our bodies. That same Christ of God rose in Paul. It seems to me that Paul wrote his letters from his experience on the road to Damascus. He came to understand what was happening to him primarily from the writings of the prophets Malachi and Isaiah. He was both Malachi's messenger of the New Covenant and Isaiah's suffering servant as an apostle. He was a Christ of God.

The authors of the four Gospels followed Paul's comment, "All who are led by the Spirit of God are the offspring of God whereby we cry, 'Abba, Father.'" As I see it, like Paul, the authors took on the Christ of God, walking in newness of the life of God. They were Christs of God in the same way Jesus and Paul and the disciples were Christs of God. They wrote from their experience, illuminated by the writings of the authors as they put on the Christ of God, walking in newness of the life of God. As they studied scriptures, they found verses corresponding with their experience of the Christ of God. The parables, the instructions, the miracles, and the words attributed to Jesus as a Christ of God fulfilled the prophetic predictions of the future of mankind as it was written in the Old Testament. All the Gospels based their message on this fulfillment. You who "have received Jesus, a Christ of God are complete in him. Buried with him in baptism you are risen with him through your faith in God, who raised him from the dead" (Colossians 2:6–12).

The Gospels and the Prophets

Paul wrote his letters from about AD 50 to AD 60 (Wikipedia; Title: Paul's Epistles). Mark wrote his first Gospel about 66 AD. Luke, Mathew, and John wrote their Gospels in that order, beginning about AD 75, separated by ten years between them (Wikipedia; Title: Gospel [Dating 5.1]).

Mark's opening words followed Paul's lead. Paul introduced himself as one "called to be an apostle separated unto the Gospel of God which he had promised afore by his prophets in Holy Scriptures" (Romans 1:1). The other four authors of the Gospels followed Paul's lead. Mark wrote, "The beginning of the Gospel of Jesus, the Son of God, as it is written in the prophets" (Mark 1:1). Luke wrote, "All things that are written by the prophets concerning the Son of Man shall be accomplished" (Luke 18:31). Matthew wrote about a particular event or prophecy to fulfill what was spoken of the Lord by the prophet (Matthew 1:22; 2:15, 17, 23; Strong, 1890, 373). John wrote, "We have found Jesus, a Christ of God of whom the prophets have written," followed by the comment, "It is written in the prophets, 'All shall be taught of the Christ of God'" (John 1:45; 6:45).

Paul and the other four Gospel authors based their knowledge of the Christ of God on the writings of the prophets and on the presence of Christ in their lives. Paul wrote, "Christ lives in me ... Examine yourselves, whether you be in the faith; prove to your own selves that Jesus, a Christ of God is in you" (Galatians 2:20; 2 Corinthians 13:5).

Each author wrote from his own experience of being born again as a Christ of God. In my opinion, the words attributed to Jesus in their Gospels were words spoken by the Christ of God in each of them. They envisaged their commitment to God as giving Him control of their bodies, keeping with Paul's comment, "Don't you know that your body is the temple of the Holy Spirit which is in you, which you received from God and *is not your own?*" (1 Corinthians 6:19; Malachi 3:1). The titles of the four Gospels indicated each Gospel was "the Gospel According to" the respective writer.

The Ministry of Jesus as a Christ of God

According to Mark, after the hiatus of his forty days in the wilderness, Jesus began his ministry when John the Baptist was put in prison. Jesus preached, "The time is fulfilled and the kingdom of God is at hand; repent and believe the Gospel." Paul similarly preached, "Now is the accepted time, now is the day of salvation," quoting the Isaiah's prophecy, which states, "In an acceptable time have I heard you and in the day of salvation. I will give you as a covenant to the people" (2 Corinthians 6:2; Isaiah 49:8).

To assist him in his ministry, Jesus called Peter, Andrew, and Zebedee's two sons, James and John, who walked away from their lives as fishermen to become fishers of men. The identification of Christians with the symbol of the fish developed after Nero's edict of persecution of the Christians, whom he blamed for the burning of Rome in AD 64.

The letters for the word "fish" correspond with the first letters of the Greek words for "Jesus, Christ, God, Son, Savior," namely "*ichthus*," as in "ichthyology" (Mark 1:17; Wikipedia, Title: Early Christian Symbol of the Fish).

Jesus led them to Capernaum, where he entered the synagogue on the Sabbath. Jesus taught them as one who had authority in accordance with Isaiah's prophecy: "All your children shall be taught of the Lord" (Isaiah 54:13). Paul reflected Isaiah with his comment, "As you have received the Christ of God, Jesus, the Lord, so you should walk in him, rooted and built upon him, established in the faith as you have been taught, abounding therein with thanksgiving" (Colossians 2:6).

Jesus's first individual healing took place in the synagogue. A man with an unclean spirit, which recognized Jesus as the "Holy One of God," asked if he had come to destroy unclean spirits. Jesus rebuked him, telling him to come out of the man. The unclean spirit *tore* the man and came out of him then (Mark 1:15–26).

Chapter Six

The Call of God

Healings and Cleansings

In my opinion, Mark's description of the first healing connected it with the prophecy of Hosea: "God has torn us and he will heal us. On the third day he will raise us up" (Hosea 6:2). This healing was also connected with Malachi's prophecy about the sun of righteousness rising with healing on his wings as well as Paul's statement quoting Hosea about the resurrection on the third day. The latter connection tied a healing to the resurrection of the dead on the third day.

The second individual healing indicated the severity of the uncleanness or sickness was unimportant. Jesus and his companions went from the synagogue to Peter's home to find Peter's mother-in-law sick with a fever. Jesus went to her, took her by the hand, and raised her up. One can only imagine why she became sick in the first place. Either she was living in his house or Peter was living in her house. In either case, she had charge of the kitchen. Her fever may have been caused be Peter's bringing home four other men for dinner without conferring with her first. Jesus's care and concern for her made her well again.

The next morning, Jesus went off by himself to pray for guidance as to what he should do next. The others followed later, and Peter advised Jesus that all men were seeking for him. "He said unto them, 'Let us go into the next towns, so I may preach there also; for this came I forth'"

(Mark 1:38). He then went to the synagogues throughout Galilee. I see Jesus's sojourn through the towns of Galilee as reminiscent of the Ark of the Covenant's moving through the tribes of Israel each month. Mark reflected the role Jesus played as Malachi's messenger of the covenant.

In one town, a leper came to Jesus and asked the Lord to make him clean. Jesus, moved with compassion, touched him and said, "I will, be thou clean." This was the third healing/cleansing. So many people sought for Jesus that he no longer could enter the cities and he had to minister to desert places. He did again go to Capernaum; however, when it was known that he was in "the house," many gathered, and the place became so packed that the crowd pressed against the door. Friends bringing a paralytic to see Jesus actually had to dig a hole in the roof to witness his ministry.

Mark wove into his Gospel Paul's dependence on the prophecies of Malachi. Mark referred to the involvement of Levites in the feedings following the healing of a man suffering from palsy, the fourth individual healing. To reach Jesus, the four carrying the invalid had to dig a hole in the roof to lower him into the crowded room. Actually, Mark's description reflected the burial of a dead man. Digging a hole in the roof made with dirt and logs would have created chaos in the room below. Digging a hole in the roof indicated this was more than a burial, which was further indicated when Jesus said to the paralytic, "Arise, pick up your bed, go your way and walk into your house" (Mark 2:1–12; Ephesians 5:14).

The word "arise" is the word often used in the Gospels as a reference to being raised from the dead. The connection with the Levites comes in the verses following the purification of the paralytic.

Mark next described Jesus's calling Levi, the tax collector:

> As [Jesus] passed by, he saw Levi, the son of Alphaeus, sitting at the receipt of taxes, and said unto him "Follow me." And he arose and followed him. And it came to pass, they sat at meat in his house; many publicans and sinners sat also together with Jesus and his disciples; for they were many and followed him. (Mark 2:14)

As in the rising of the paralytic, the Greek word translated here as "arose" has the same root of the word translated as "resurrection" in

Paul's comment about "the resurrection from the dead" (Romans 1:4). Levi's call was a repetition of the calling of the first four disciples. Like them, Jesus called for Levi to follow him. Without asking any questions, Levi walked away from his livelihood just as the first four disciples had. Levi invited them to his house for dinner.

The Romans did not collect taxes. They sold the right to gather taxes on sections of the highways to the native people for whatever they could get from travelers passing through their area. The Jews looked at them as traitors doing the work of Rome and put them in the class of sinners and Gentiles. When the scribes and Pharisees questioned why Jesus ate with them, Jesus replied, "Those who are whole have no need of the physician. But those who are sick [need one]. I came not to call righteous [people], but [I came] to call sinners to repentance" (Mark 2:17).

The Pharisees went on to ask Jesus why his disciples didn't fast as John the Baptist's and the Pharisees' disciples had. His answer was that the bridegroom was with them and fasting was inappropriate, reflecting Paul's statement, "He had espoused them to one husband to the Christ of God" (Mark 2:18; 2 Corinthians 11:2). Jesus went on to say, "No man sews a piece of new cloth to an old garment. And no man puts new wine into old bottles." Again, he reflected Paul's comment when he said, "Old things have passed away; behold, all things are new" (Mark 2:21; 2 Corinthians 5:17).

These healings laid the foundation for understanding Jesus's remarks, after the second feeding in the wilderness, about our understanding of the numbers involved in the two feedings. The healings are actually purifications of the Jews and the Gentiles. How this becomes apparent requires information about the numbering of the tribes of Israel.

The Thirteenth Tribe and the Temple of God

When Jacob was on his deathbed, he called each of his twelve sons to receive his blessing and their portion of his inheritance. He called Joseph first and told him to bring with him his two sons, Ephraim and Manasseh. Jacob thereupon adopted Joseph's two sons, declaring the tribe of Joseph would be known by the names of his two sons, making Joseph's inheritance double the portion of the inheritance given the other tribes (Genesis 48:1–22).

The Book of Numbers began with a census of the tribes of Israel. The census of the tribe of Joseph consisted of two censuses – one of Ephraim and one of Manasseh. However, the tribes of Israel were still referred to as twelve in number. Why? God directed that the Levites were not to be numbered as a tribe of Israel. *They were appointed to care for the tabernacle and all its vessels* (Numbers 1:49–53; 3:12–17; 4:1). God declared, "I have taken the Levites from among the children of Israel to take the place of all the firstborn sons who open the matrix among the children of Israel. The Levites shall be mine" (Exodus 13:2–12; Numbers 3:12). God also declared, "The tribe of Levi shall have no part nor inheritance with Israel. *The Lord God is his inheritance.*"

> This shall be the (Levitical) priests' due from the people, from them that offer sacrifice, whether it be ox or sheep. You shall *give* to them the shoulder, the two cheeks, and the maw with the first fruit also of your corn, of the wine, and of your oil; and the first fleece of your sheep shall you give them. (Deuteronomy 18:1–4)

We have already seen how Malachi has been the prophet most relied on by Paul and the Gospels. Malichi accused the Levities of failing to insist the sacrifices be the best of the animals and fruits and not the sick and rotten food. Malachi is the basis for Christians's taking on the Levite's role of caring for the temple of God in place of the Jews. The healing miracles are purification. Malachi quoted God by saying the following:

> My covenant is with Levi. My covenant of life and peace was with Levi who feared for my name. The messenger of the covenant (Christ), in whom you delight, *shall purify the sons of the Levites like a refiner's fire and fuller's soap.* He shall sit as a refiner and Levi shall then come as a purifier of silver, he shall purify them as gold and silver so that they may offer unto the Lord an offering [of service as the Christ of God] in righteousness. Those who feared for the Lord and thought upon his name shall be mine. I will spare them as a man spares his own son who serves him The day of the Lord comes burning as an oven for those who choose not to serve

God. And unto you who fear for my name shall the Sun of Righteousness rise with healing on his wings. You shall go forth as calves left out of the stall. (Malachi 1:4; 3:1–3, 16; 4:2)

We are called to be the temple of God, the messengers of the covenant, purified to be Levites caring for our bodies as dwelling places of God. We become the heirs of God supplanting the Jews, who live by the law and ordinances. We are more than the people of God. We are the offspring of God (Romans 7:10–8:30). Paul wrote of the exchange of Christians for the Levites in place of the Jews in his remark, "Have they [the Jews] stumbled that they should fall? God forbid … Through their fall, salvation is come to the Gentiles" (Romans 11:11).

Mark may have pulled a sleight of hand. Jesus's call to Levi to follow him is the only mention of Levi, the tax collector. His name appears in the Gospel of Mark. Mark was originally named John. He changed it to Mark when he joined with Paul. His uncle Barnabas was originally named Joses. He was a Levite, which means Mark had to be a Levite too, because they were part of the same family (Acts 4:36). Mark isn't listed as an apostle, although his brother is on the list (Mark 3:14–19). Mark was aware that those who became followers of Paul were mostly converts of the gates. Mark knew that in the future these converts would dominate Christianity as the inheritors of the role of caring for the temple of God in themselves, who are the Christians in our time. I think Mark cast himself in the role of the unlisted apostle named Levi.

The Show Bread

Mark next focused on the loaves of showbread in the story of the time when the disciples plucked wheat seed on the Sabbath. The Pharisees accused Jesus of disobeying the commandment to keep the Sabbath day holy. In reply, Jesus said the following:

Have you never read what David did, when he had need and was hungry? How he went into the house of God and did eat the showbread which is not lawful to eat but for the priests [including the Levites under their charge] and gave also to them who were with him. The Sabbath was made for man and not man for the Sabbath. (Mark 2:25)

God gave the charge of the Levites to Aaron and his priesthood, entitling the Levites to eat the shewbread. The Levites wholly belonged to God, but they were separated from any listing of the twelve tribes of Israel (Numbers 3:9, 12). There were thirteen tribes of Israel made up of the twelve listed (Numbers 1:1–15, 49–53), plus the tribe of Levi, who belonged to God (Numbers 8:11–16). God instructed Moses to bake twelve loaves of bread to be put in two rows of six at each end of the table. Every Sabbath, the bread was to be replaced with fresh loaves. The bread was called the shewbread, because it showed the care and presence of God in the wilderness (Leviticus 24:5–9; Exodus 25:30). According to Paul, just as the shewbread fed the Israelites in the desert, the bread we break in the service of Holy Communion is the communion of the body of Christ (1 Corinthians 10:16–18).

Jesus's comment about David's eating the shewbread developed when David had to flee from King Saul's intent to have him (David) killed. David fled with four supporters to Nob, where Ahimelech, the son of Abiathar, the high priest, was serving as a priest. David asked for and received five loaves of bread for him and his men, who had not eaten for three days. There was no common bread at hand, so Ahimelech gave him five loaves of the shewbread on the altar (1 Samuel 21:1–7).

The shewbread represented the presence of God. Jesus was filled with the life of God, which meant that the disciples were feeding on the presence of God in Jesus as they were eating the wheat in the field. The wheat sustained their living the lives of God, stimulated by God's presence in Jesus just as it had sustained David and his men to avoid assassination at the hands of King Saul, saving the establishment of kingdom of Israel under David. After the rebuke of the Pharisees, Mark described Jesus's visit to the synagogue, where he healed a man with a withered hand on the Sabbath. This was the fifth healing.

The objection of the Pharisees to Jesus's work on the Sabbath led Jesus to ask, "Is it lawful to do good on the Sabbath day, or to do evil?" Jesus's question was in keeping with Paul's message about God's life having precedence over obedience to the law (Mark 3:4; 2 Corinthians 3:3). Jesus looked at the Pharisees with anger for the hardness of their hearts. Jesus healed the man's hand, whereupon the Pharisees "took council with the Herodians how they might destroy Jesus" (Mark 3:1–8).

A great multitude from Galilee, Judea, and Jerusalem as well as beyond Jordan followed Jesus. Jesus took his followers up a mountain. He ordained twelve, who would be with him and whom he would send to preach and to have power to heal sicknesses and cast out demons (Mark 3:13).

The disciples' ability to heal the sick and cast out demons indicated they, too, were the Christs of God as Jesus was. This miraculous ability had also been attributed to Paul (Acts 14:8–11). The list of disciples began with the first four called—Peter, James, John, and Andrew. One would expect to find Levi as the fifth, calling among the eight other people and completing the twelve that represented the tribes of Israel. Levi could not be counted, however, because he had been separated from the tribes to take care of the temple (Numbers 1:49).

By this omission, Mark emphasized Levi was one of the disciples not to be counted in any numbering of the tribes of Israel. The thirteen disciples represented the twelve tribes of Israel, who were thirteen in number but referred to as twelve. Levi's omission from the list of the disciples and his taking the place of the first-born sons of all Jewish births, together with his being the one with whom God would make His New Covenant, suggests Levi represented all who would be born of God in the years to come. I believe, Mark intended to convey that the Levites represented the Christians in every future generation called to be the temple of God. Mark ws born about the time Jesus began his ministry Christians so he was like those who didn't know Jesus.

The Christians

The feedings in the wilderness were two in number, according to the Old Testament, one in the Book of Exodus (16:11–27) and the other in the Book of Numbers (11:31–35). The first feeding was instigated by the murmurings of the children of Israel (Exodus 16:12). The second feeding developed out of the cries of a mixed multitude, meaning Gentiles, who joined the children of Israel in the wilderness according to Numbers 11:4.

The Bible identified these two groups of converts. The Gentile converts of righteousness obeyed all the laws and commandments. The number seven indicated a mixed multitude made up of converts of the gates who observed the Sabbath but were selective as to the ordinances and commandments. The converts of the gates, also known as the "God fearers," were welcome to worship on the Sabbath with the first group. However, the Jews and the converts of righteousness would not eat with them nor would they go into their houses.

After the appointment of the disciples, Mark raised the question of where Jesus stood with regard to these two groupings. Jesus's family and friends thought Jesus was out of his mind. Scribes came from Jerusalem and accused him of casting out the demons, because they thought Beelzebub had possessed him. In reply, Jesus said, "A kingdom, divided against itself, cannot stand." Jesus's brethren and his mother came to get him. They stood outside, sending others to call him out. They would not go in, because they were devout Jews and Jesus was meeting with publicans and sinners (Mark 3:21–35). Jesus's answer to their call rejected his family, and according to Mark, he said:

> "Who is my mother and brethren?" And he looked at those who sat round about him, and said, "Behold my mother and my brethren. For whosoever shall do the will of God is my brother and sister mother. (Mark 3:33)

Paul said much the same thing when he wrote, "Be transformed by the renewing of your mind so that you may prove what is that good and acceptable will of God. We, being many, are one body in .the Christ of God, and everyone members of one another" (Romans 12:2–5)

All who did the will of God were Jesus's family and have God as their father. They were the children of God just as Jesus was a Son of God. Three chapters later, Mark wrote, "A prophet is not without honor, except in his own country, among his own kin, and in his own house." Mark may have been speaking of his own situation as well as Paul's.

Both of them came from devout Jewish families. The early followers of Jesus met in Mark's mother's house (Acts 12:12). She put him through the study of the commandments and ordinances under the Pharisees at the temple. Paul was in the same situation.

His family paid for his early years of study with tutors and later in the temple when he became an adult. In the years of his ministry, he never had any success in his hometown. *He spent some time in Tarsus when he had to flee Damascus, and the fellowship of Jesus's followers in Jerusalem would not receive him then* (Acts 9:20–30). His missionary journeys took him through Tarsus a couple of times. It is hard to imagine that Paul didn't preach there. He had no success as far as we know.

Jesus began to teach the multitudes from a ship on the Sea of Galilee. His first teaching was a parable about how a seed's growth depended on the kind of ground upon which it fell. The seed sown on good ground represented those who received the word of God and cultivated it to bring forth fruit as much as a hundredfold, providing both seed for the sowers and bread for the eaters (Mark 4:1–32). Mark's description paralleled Paul's comment in his letter to the Corinthians about how God's supplying seed to the sower ministers bread for food and multiplies your seed to increase the fruits of righteousness (2 Corinthians 9:10). Paul's comment paralleled Isaiah's prophecy about the rain and snow watering the earth to make it bring forth and bud so that it may give seed to the sower and bread to the eater (Isaiah 55:10). Paul identified the seed as the Christ of God (Galatians 3:16).

Jesus went on to sail across the Sea of Galilee to the land of the Gadarenes. On the way, a great storm of wind arose. The waves swamped the ship. The disciples woke Jesus, and he calmed the storm, allowing them to pass safely to the opposite side (Mark 4:35–41). This story reflected the experience of Paul on his trip to Rome when his ship was caught in a storm off the island of Malta. Paul took charge of the situation, and all were saved as the crew followed his suggestions, although the ship was wrecked when it grounded (Acts 27: 1–44).

When Jesus reached the eastern shore of the Sea of Galilee, a man with an unclean spirit met them. He had been living among the tombs. He had been bounded with fetters and chains, which he tore asunder. He was continually cutting himself on the stones. When he saw Jesus, he ran and worshipped him. Jesus said to the unclean spirit, "Come out of the man." In reply to Jesus's asking its name, the unclean spirit answered, "My name is legion, for we are many." There was a great herd of swine feeding, and all the devils of the unclean spirit asked Jesus to let them go into the swine. Jesus gave them leave to do so. The unclean spirits, which were about two thousand in number, went into the herd and then ran down a steep place into the sea and drowned. Those tending the swine told the city and the countryside what had happened. They were afraid when they found the demoniac in his right mind. They pleaded with Jesus to depart from their coasts (Mark 5:1–17).

The healing of the demoniac had many similarities with the freedom of the Jews from bondage when they escaped from Egypt. They were enslaved then, making bricks for the tombs and other buildings for the pharaoh. The sharp edges of the bricks cut their hands. In the first century, the word "legion" referred to the Roman army. The army of the pharaohs drowned in the waters of the Red Sea, too. The Roman Army acted like pigs when they conquered an area. They took the best land for themselves. They taxed the defeated populations. They commandeered animals and harvests.

The next two healings—number seven and eight—involved two daughters of Israel. When Jesus passed to the west side of the Sea of Galilee, the ruler of a synagogue met him and implored him to come and lay his hands on his daughter. She was at the point of death. Jesus went with him, followed by a multitude of people. Among the throng accompanying them was a woman who suffered from an issue of blood for the past twelve years at the hands of many physicians. She had spent all that she had, but she had only grown worse. She thought if she touched Jesus's garment, she would be made whole.

After she pressed through the throng, she touched his clothes, and the issue of blood stopped instantly. Jesus knew immediately virtue had passed from him and he asked who had touched him. The woman was fearful. She fell down at his feet and confessed to what she had done. Jesus comforted her and said, "Daughter, your faith has made you whole; go in peace free of your plague." While Jesus spoke, word came from the ruler of the synagogue's house with the news that his daughter was dead (Mark 5:25–34).

Taking only Peter, James, and John, Jesus followed the ruler to his house to find it in a tumult of great wailing and weeping. Jesus said, "Why make this ado? The child is not dead; she is asleep." The mourners laughed at him. Jesus then followed the child's parents to where she was lying, took her by the hand, and said to her, "Damsel, arise," whereupon she arose and walked, for she was twelve years old. Jesus went on to direct that she be fed (Mark 5:21–24, 35–43).

The length of twelve years for the sickness of the elder woman and the age of the child indicated these were healings of Jews. They represented the older and younger Jews. All the healings thus far were healings of Jews, mostly taking place in the synagogues or in areas inhabited by Jews, such as the land of the Gadarenes (the Tribe of Gad). Those who were healed came to Jesus seeking help, or they were brought to him by family or friends. In the case of the unclean spirits, they revealed themselves for what they were. The unclean spirits tore themselves from the possessed persons, whom Jesus told to go in peace or to take up their bed and walk or to arise or to go and sin no more or to be cleansed.

The need for us to choose to be cleansed came from Paul's epistles when he wrote a paraphrase of Deuteronomy (30:10–15, 19):

> Say not in your heart, "Who shall ascend into heaven to bring Christ down? Who shall descend into the deep to bring Christ from the dead." The word is even in your mouth and in your heart. Whoever shall call upon the name of the Lord shall be saved. (Romans 10:6–9, 13)

Paul substituted the word "Christ" for the word 'word' in Deuteronomy, which ended with this observation: "I [God] have set before you both life and death, blessing and curse, therefore choose life, so that *you and your seed may live*" (Deuteronomy 30:19).

After the eighth healing, Jesus sent the disciples two by two probably so each could be encouraged by feeding on the presence of God in each other and could report on their accomplishments to preach repentance for the forgiveness of sin. The disciples cast out many devils and healed the sick, anointing them with oil, validating the power given to them when Jesus earlier appointed them as disciples (Mark 6:7–13).

Word came that Herod had John the Baptist executed at the request of his daughter. The news led Jesus to take the disciples to a desert place to rest a while "because many were coming and going and had no time to eat. (Mark6:31) A multitude of people gathered around Jesus and his disciples and followed them when they crossed over the Sea Galilee to a desert place. Jesus was moved with compassion toward them because "they were sheep without shepherd" now that John was killed. (Mark 6:34; Numbers 27:16f).

Jesus began to teach them many things. When the day was far spent, Jesus directed his disciples to feed the people with the five loaves and two small fish. They all ate, and they were filled. They took up twelve baskets of fragments of bread and fish. The multitude numbered about five thousand. Jesus then became the leader of those who followed John's preaching (Mark: 6:33–44).

Jesus sent the disciples back to the other shore in the boat. During the fourth watch, Jesus saw them laboring with the wind against them. Then Jesus walked on the sea as if to pass them by; however, they cried out to him, and he went over to them. The wind ceased. When they landed on the shore, wherever they went, people brought the sick, hoping they might just touch the border of his garment (Mark 6:46–56).

Pharisees and scribes came from Jerusalem to see what was happening. They complained about the disciples eating bread without washing their hands. Jesus answered them with a quote from Isaiah: "These people honor me [God] with their lips but their heart is far from me; they worship me in vain, teaching for doctrines the commandments of men" (Isaiah 29:13). Paul made a similar remark to Colossians: "[God] has forgiven you all your trespasses, blotting out the handwriting on the ordinances which were against us and nailing it to his cross" (Colossians 2:13).

Jesus next went into the borders of Tyre and Sidon by himself without letting anyone know. A woman whose daughter had an unclean spirit heard of his presence. She sought him out to ask him to heal her daughter. She was a Greek, a Syrophenician. Jesus said to her, "Let the children first be filled; for it is not meet to take the children's bread and cast it out to dogs." She answered, "Yes, Lord, yet the dogs under the table eat of the children's crumbs." Jesus then said to her, "Go your way, the devil has gone out of your daughter When the mother returned to her house, she found her daughter free of the devil. This was the ninth healing (Mark 7:24–30).Jesus took the long way back to Capernaum. He went northeast of the Sea of Galilee to the Decapolis cities, which were populated with Gentiles like Tyre and Sidon were. While he was in the area, Jesus healed a man, probably a Greek, who was deaf and had an impediment in his speech. This was the tenth healing (Mark 7:31–37).

The Bread of the Christ of God

Upon Jesus's return to Galilee, a great multitude again gathered around him in the wilderness for three days without anything to eat. The disciples had seven loaves of bread and a few small fish, which Jesus blessed and gave to his disciples to set before the people. The crowd was about four thousand in number. Seven baskets were gathered (Mark 8:1–9). The seven loaves used in the second feeding sugested that with the five loaves of the first feeding the twelve loaves represented the twelve loaves set on the altar in the temple.

Jesus dismissed the multitude, and with his disciples, he set out in a ship on the Sea of Galilee. The disciples forgot to take bread with them, yet they had one loaf with them in the boat. Jesus made a remark about the leaven of the Pharisees and Herod, which confused the disciples. The disciples reasoned that he was referring to their forgetting to bring bread. When Jesus knew it, he said, "Why do you reason because you have no bread? Don't you yet perceive or understand. Is your heart hardened?" (Mark 8:10–21).

It was not clear whether or not they had bread with them. Twice Mark wrote they had no bread, yet he also wrote they had one loaf, which probably referred to Jesus. It seems to me that the five loaves used in the first feeding are a reference to the five loaves of showbread given to David and the four others with him. The five loaves also coincided with the first five people called to follow Jesus. The twelve baskets of fragments indicated the feeding was limited to the people of Israel who were cleansed as they fed on the bread of Christ.

The five thousand persons fed at the first feeding reflected the same idea that the number those fed coincided with the first five to be called to follow Jesus and feed on the presence of God in their lives. This is also true of the number of people who fed on the presence of God at the second feeding. There was an additional four thousand which brought the total number to nine thousand. At this point there had been ten purification miracles one of which was not to be counted bringing the number down to nine. The one not to be counted was the daughter of the Greek mother who was healed out of time like Levi.

I think Mark is saying that to be born again as a child of God we must let go of the 'they' world to become as unblemished as a chaste virgin because for us to be the dwelling place of God in keeping with Paul's statement to that effect (2 Corinthians 11:3) Just seeking out to change one's life is evidence of our accepting the fore-giveness of God, the future of His being (Matthew 7:6f; John 16:23-27). Jesus never said, "I forgive you." He recognized power of the Holy Spirit's passing into another person as in the case of the woman with an issue of blood. There was no more showbread to feed a multitude. The seven baskets of fragments represented the seven thousand who ate the showbread. When Mark introduced the second feeding in the wilderness, the multitude had been in the wilderness for three days without anything to eat. The three days without food is probably a reference to the resurrection's taking place on the third day. Jesus, a Christ of God, was the seed of God, which He breathed into the first man, Adam (Genesis 2:7). Adam's seed of God multiplied in succeeding generations. That multiplication was predicted to occur in those who would choose the everlasting covenant God offered to them. Their seed would bear a hundred fold according to Mark's parable of the sowing of the seed, which he attributed to Jesus:

> Behold there went out a sower to sow. As he sowed some fell by the way side and the fowls of the air came and devoured it. Some fell on stony ground where it had not much earth. It immediately sprang up, because it had no depth of earth. But when the sun was up, it was scorched and because it had not root it withered away. Some fell among thorns, and the thorns grew up, and choked it, and it yielded no fruit. Other fell on good ground and yielded fruit that sprang up and increased, and brought forth, some thirty, and some sixty and some an hundredfold. (Mark 4:3–8; Isaiah 55:10)

Mark's parable was first introduced in Paul's comments to the Corinthians, "Now he who ministers seed to the sower both ministers bread for your food and multiply your seed sown, and increase the fruits of your righteousness," (2Corinthians9:10) and to the Galatians., "Now to Abraham and his seed were the promises made. He did not say, 'And to seeds,' as though there were many kinds of seeds, but to the one seed in you—which is the seed of Christ" (Galatians 3:16).

Another source for Mark's parable of the sower was Isaiah's proclamation about his anointment ("christening" in the Septuagint) to preach the Gospel unto the meek, to bind up the broken hearted, to proclaim liberty to the captives and the opening of the prison to them who were bound. Isaiah went on to comment "they shall be called the planting of the Lord" (Isaiah 61:1–3).

> They shall be called trees of righteousness, planting, of the Lord, so that God might be glorified. I [God] will direct their work in truth. I will make with them an everlasting covenant (Isaiah 61:3–9). [As for me] I will greatly rejoice in the Lord, my soul shall be joyful in my God; for he hath clothed me with the garments of salvation, he hath covered me with the robe of righteousness, as a bridegroom decks himself with ornaments and as a bride adorns herself with her jewels (Isaiah 61:10) … For as young man marries a virgin, so shall [God's] children marry Him [God]; and as the bridegroom rejoices over the bride, so shall your God rejoice over you. (Isaiah 62:5; 2 Corinthians 11:2)

> This is my covenant with you, my spirit and my words which I have put in your mouth, shall not depart away from you, nor away from your seed, nor from the mouth of your seeds' seed. (Isaiah 59:21–60:1)

Isaiah's prophecy pictured a joyous spiritual bonding between God and an unblemished human, wherein there was no male or female, no Jew or Gentiles, no slave or freeman, only, as far as the human was concerned, care-fullness for the well-being of everyone and everything. God and the human melded together as a Christ producing fruits of righteousness. That righteousness was comparable to the joy in a marriage where two find themselves on the same wave length of concern for the well-being of each other. A planting of righteousness produced both food and seed.

The fruit was food to sustain awareness of the presence and care of the Christ of God in us as he was in Jesus. Feeding on the presence and care of God ran through Mark's Gospel from beginning to end. The feeding began when Jesus healed Peter's mother-in-law so she could feed them. The calling of Levi led to Jesus's eating in his house with the disciples, publicans, and sinners. When the Pharisees asked why Jesus didn't fast with his disciples as John the Baptist had fasted, Jesus replied that the bridegroom's friends should not fast while the bridegroom, the Christ of God in Jesus, was with them.

The story of the disciples' feeding on wheat as they passed near a grain field on the Sabbath was analogous to David and his men's feeding on the showbread, which represented the presence and care of God in the daily supply of manna God provided in the wilderness. The parable of the sowing of the seed on bad and good ground led Jesus to compare the kingdom of God to a mustard seed planted into the ground, producing additional seed well over a hundredfold (Mark 4:26–32). The two feedings in the wilderness, one of five thousand and the other of four thousand people, sustained them on the seed of the presence of the Christ of God in Jesus and his disciples.

Luke (4:1–14), followed by Matthew (4:1–11), grasped this scenario of these feeding in the wilderness. They described the temptations the devil put before Jesus in his forty-day sojourn in the desert. The first temptation was the devil's suggestion that Jesus make stones into bread to prove he was the son of God. Jesus silenced him with a quotation from Deuteronomy (8:3) regarding the manna, which God fed to the Jews during their forty-year sojourn in the wilderness: "Man does not live by bread alone; rather, he lives by *every word* which proceeds from the mouth of the Lord (Yahweh)."

As previously shown, Paul identified the word of God as the Christ of God. God expressed Himself as Christ by His word just as we express ourselves by the words we breathe out of our mouths. The six-day story of the creation of the universe and everything in it portrays the universe as an expression of God through His word, including a child born of God. Its conception takes place when the seed sown in every human being, both male and female through evolution, is stimulated by the word of God calling us to choose the carefulness road of righteousness.

The disciples were confused by Jesus's suggestion that the numbers involved in the two feedings had some significance. The numbers didn't make any sense. How did five or twelve loaves of bread feed thousands of people? It was done by the fulfillment of God's promise to Abraham to "multiply his seed as the stars of the heavens and as the sand upon the sea shore." The fulfillment was the result of their sharing the life of God with one another under the stimulus of the presence of Jesus and the disciples (Genesis 22:17f).

The fulfillment of the seed's multiplication also lay behind Isaiah's comment about God's marriage to a virgin (Isaiah 61:3, 6, 8, 10; 62:5). The same fulfillment lay behind Paul's declaration, "I have espoused you to one husband, so that I may present you as a chaste virgin to Christ" (2 Corinthians 11:2). Luke used a wording similar to Paul's when he wrote about the conception of Jesus (Luke 1:20–35). Matthew announced Mary's conception as a virgin espoused to Joseph in a dream based on the prophecy of first Isaiah (7:14; 9:2–6): "A virgin shall be with child and shall bring forth a son, and they shall call his name Emmanuel, which means 'God with us.'" John tied the beginning of Jesus's ministry with a wedding "on the third day," indicating the wedding marked the beginning of Jesus's ministry and our espousal with God's life through Jesus, starting with the purification jars of water.

Espoused to God

The connection of God as our husband stemmed from the opening story of Adam and Eve. They became one flesh (Genesis 2:24). As husband and wife, they passed on to their offspring the seed of God's self, which He breathed into Adam and which passed on to Eve through the bone and flesh of Adam. As we have already seen, Isaiah made a similar statement, followed by the basis for multiplying God's seed:

> *Your Maker is your husband* ... Incline your ear, and come unto me [God]. Listen and your soul shall live. I will make with you an everlasting covenant (Isaiah 54:1–4; 55:3, 10) ... For as the rain comes down, and the snow from heaven, watering the earth and making it bud, so that it may give seed to the sower and bread

to the eater, thus shall my word be which goes out of my mouth. It shall not return unto me void, but it shall accomplish that which I please. It shall prosper where I have sent it. You shall go out with joy, and be led forth with peace. The mountains and hills will burst into singing, and the trees of the field shall clap their hands. (Isaiah 54:3–55:10)

Isaiah's comments about the multiplication of the seed are also the basis of the parable of the sower in Mark (4:1–34), Luke (8:4–15), and Matthew (13:1–23). The same multiplication of the seed lies in the last chapter of Isaiah when he writes, "Shall I [God] bring to birth and shut the womb? (Isaiah 66:9)."

The multiplication of the seed of the self of God developed out of God's sowing the seed of Himself in Adam. The self of God was seeded in every human in a dormant state. At his baptism, Jesus committed himself to live his life as a child of God. Jesus was then anointed with the self of God. The disciples and the multitudes were similar offspring of the Lord God, as they fed on the seed of God emanating from the face of Jesus. Paul put it this way, "Since by man came death, by man also came the resurrection of the dead. In Adam all died. In the Christ of God, all shall be made alive" (1 Corinthians 15:20f).

The seed of God's life radiated from Jesus: "For God who commanded the light to shine in the darkness shined in our hearts to give the light of the knowledge of God in the face of Jesus Christ" (2 Corinthians 4:6). The seed of the Christ of God in Jesus awakened in the disciples, presenting them with an option to be as one with the self of God as Jesus was. When they accepted the future will of God's being (God's fore-giveness) to walk the path of His righteousness, they gave up their dead lives in the 'they' world. The life of God emanated from their faces as they produced the fruits of righteousness. They took on God's self as they let go of the self of alienation from His life. Even though it happened to the disciples as they followed in Jesus's footsteps they weren't aware of its significance, "they did not consider the miracles of the loaves [after the first feeding] for their hearts were hardened" (Mark 6:52).

Jesus tried again after the second feeding when they found themselves without bread in the boat. Jesus said, "Why do you reason because you have no bread? Don't you perceive what has happened? Neither do you understand? Have you still hardened hearts?" (Mark 8:17). Then Jesus reviewed the numbers of loaves and baskets of fragments in the two feedings of the multitudes. He closed with the question, "How is it that you do not understand?" What was it they didn't understand? In spite of their power to heal and baptize people on their own and feed crowds in the wilderness, they did not realize they were Christs of God as Jesus was.

Mark next described the eleventh healing miracle of a blind man, suggesting that the disciples were blind to what was happening to them. They could not conceive the Christ of God was in them as it was in Jesus. At the feedings, Jesus did not distribute any bread, because he wanted them to see that the disciples and the people were the ones who spread the seed of God. Before the first feeding, he had ordained the twelve disciples to be with him to send them forth to preach the Gospel, with the power of the presence of God's seed in them to heal sicknesses and cast out demons (Mark 3:15). They still didn't understand they had the power as Christs to do what Jesus could do. This was followed by the story about Jesus's family being those who fulfilled the will of God (Mark 3:31–34).

Mark next described Jesus's healings of the daughter of Israel (Mark 5:38–42) and the daughter of a Gentile (Mark 7:24–30), suggesting the seed of God's life should be available to all the nations of the world through the disciples' sharing of the seed of the presence of God. Jesus sent the disciples out in pairs so that one could see the other fulfilling the role of the Christ in themselves and not just in Jesus.

According to Mark, the multiplication of bread and the fruits of righteousness spread through the multitudes. In turn, the disciples were the source of the seed for the rest of the multitude, with whom they shared what bread they had. The disciples and multitudes were raised from the dead to live in unity with God. The fruits of righteousness were the seeds, which sustained their life in God and, in turn, passed that life down from generation to generation.

Jesus was trying to enlighten the disciples about their bearing fruits of righteousness as both food for body and as food to stir up the seed of the life of God already sown in them. In the Gospel of Mark, Jesus stressed over and over again that he was a human being. Throughout his Gospel, Mark wrote of Jesus as a "Son of Man" and not as the "Son of God," even though God and the unclean spirits recognized him in the latter role. Use of the "Son of Man" title not only stressed Jesus's humanity but also suggested this was the destiny of all mankind, namely bearing fruits of righteous. Mark wrote the following:

> Jesus began to teach them that the Son of Man must suffer many things, and be rejected of the elders, and of the chief priests and scribes and be killed and after three days rise again. Peter took Jesus aside and began to rebuke Jesus. Jesus then turned to rebuke Peter in the face of the other disciples saying, "Get behind me Satan for you do not savor the things of God, but the things of Man." (Mark 8:31–32)

Luke reported a similar incident about Paul's rebuke of Peter (Galatians 2:9–13).

The scenario Mark presented reflected Paul's understanding of the prophet Hosea with regard to the resurrection on the third day. The resurrection was necessary, because God had torn and smitten the Israelites to death. God had cut them to pieces (hewed them) by the prophets. He had slain them with His words, for God desired mercy and not sacrifice, and the knowledge of God more than burnt offerings. They had broken the covenant and dealt treacherously against God. Like troops of robbers, so the company of priests had murdered as highway men, men who made any trip dangerous (Hosea 5:14; 6:9). God had seen Israel's fathers as the first ripened (fruit) on the fig tree at her first time (Hosea 9:10). When Israel was a child, God had loved him and called His son out of Egypt (Hosea 11:1).

Fruits of Righteousness

Jesus led mankind into living the life of God. God's will dwelled in them. His life was the destiny to which every human is called by the presence of the seed of the self of God in us. We are destined to bring forth fruits of righteousness, triggering a similar reaction in those who accept the forgiveness of God as we give up the life of alienation from

God. Paul's prayer for the well-being of the Colossians gives us this overview while he revealed his own life in his remarks to Galatians:

> The truth of the Gospel has come unto you, as it is in the entire world, and brings forth fruit. We do not cease to desire that you might be filled with the knowledge of [God's] will in all wisdom and spiritual understanding so that you might walk worthy of the Lord unto all patience and long suffering with joyfulness, giving thanks unto the Father which has made us meet [eligible] to be partakers of the inheritance of the saints in light, who has delivered us unto the kingdom of His dear Son. In him we have redemption through his blood, even the forgiveness of sin. You, who were alienated and enemies in your mind by wicked works, now has He reconciled in the body of his flesh through death [on the cross] to present you holy [purified] in His sight. (Colossians 1:5–22)

> I am crucified with the Christ of God. Yet, I live. But it is not I who lives; it is the Christ of God who lives in me. The life I now live in the flesh, I live by the faith of the Son of God, who loved me and gave himself for me. (Galatians 2:20)

According to Mark, the failure of the disciples to recognize the Holy Spirit dwelling in them as it dwelt in Jesus became apparent in Mark's description of how Jesus abruptly changed the direction of his service as the "Messenger of the New Covenant." After he healed the blind man (the eleventh miracle), Jesus went with his disciples to the cities of Caesarea Philippi. On the way, the Bible indicated they had the following conversation:

> "Who do men say that I am?" They answered, "Some say John the Baptist, or Elijah, or one of the prophets." Jesus went on to ask, "But who do you say that I am?" Peter answered, "You are the Christ." Jesus then began to teach them the Son of man must suffer many things; he would be rejected of the elders and of the chief priests,

and scribes, and be killed. After three days rise again.
(Mark 8:27–31)

The change of direction warrants a reminder of the basis for Paul and Mark's understandings of the Gospel of God. Both based their understandings on the writings of prophets in the scriptures of the Old Testament. They were not writing about the life of Jesus. They were writing about the Christ of God in Jesus and in themselves. Jesus recognized the disciples were so hardened by the traditions of Judaism that they could not conceive of themselves as Christs of God. At best, they believed Jesus was their shepherd, leading them on the path of the righteousness of God. They did not understand that God dwelled in all living the life of God.

Paul listed what it meant to live the life of God:

> Though I speak with the tongues of men and of angels, and have not charity, I am as sounding brass, or a tinkling cymbal. Though I have the gift of prophecy and understand all mysteries, and all knowledge; and though I have all faith, so that I could move mountains, and have not charity, I am nothing. Though I bestow all my goods to feed the poor and though I give my body to be burned, and have not charity, it profits me nothing. Charity suffers long, and is kind. Charity envies not. Charity vaunts not itself, is not puffed up. [Charity] does not behave itself unseemly, seeks not its own, is not provoked, thinks no evil. [Charity] rejoices not in iniquity, but rejoices in truth. Charity bears all things, believes all things, hopes all things, and endures all things…. Now abides these three: faith, hope and charity, but the greatest of these is charity. (1 Corinthians 13:1–13)

The Humanity of Christ

Charity produces fruits of righteousness—doing something for anyone near us. We then are in Christ, and Christ is in us. The self of our being then radiates the being of God. Our self becomes the self of God as the being of God shines from our hearts. The Christ of God is a human, the future of whose being (i.e. the will of our being) is the future of the being of God (the will of His being) Mark understood the importance of the humanity of Jesus. Mark's reference to Jesus as a Son of Man is essential if we are to have the same being of God as Jesus had. If Jesus wasn't an ordinary, run-of-the-mill human but had some divine power we don't have, we couldn't follow in his footsteps.

Mark described Jesus's humanity a number of times in his Gospel. When the Pharisees rebuked him for letting his disciples harvest wheat on the Sabbath, Jesus looked at them with anger (Mark 2:24, 3:5). He disclaimed membership in his family when his mother and brethren sought him to come away from the multitude around him (Mark 3:31–35). The Greek mother had to shame Jesus into healing her daughter (Mark 7:27). Jesus called Peter "Satan" in front of all the disciples when Peter was considerate of Jesus, taking him aside to rebuke Jesus for teaching the disciples that the "Son of Man" would be killed at the hands of the temple hierarchy (Mark 8:31–33). When he came to Jerusalem, Jesus destroyed a fig tree with a curse when he was hungry and found no fruit on the tree, even though it wasn't the season for fruit in the first place. The fig tree was a reference to Israel (Mark 11:14; Hosea 9:10; Joel 1:7; John 1:48). He overturned the tables of the money changers and drove out those who bought and sold in the temple.

The Book of Acts described a similar instance of Paul's humanity. He refused to take Mark on the second missionary journey. Mark had left Paul and his uncle, Barnabas, on the first missionary journey after he had reached the first port on the trip. Paul wanted to go on a second journey to visit the churches they had established on the first journey. Barnabas wanted to take Mark with them, too, but Paul, in a pout, refused because Mark had left the first journey (Acts 15:36–39). Another instance of Paul's humanity parallels Jesus rebuke of Peter. Paul bragged about it in his letter to the Galatians:

> When Peter came to Antioch, Paul withstood him face to face, because he was to be blamed. For before certain men came from James, Peter ate with the Gentiles. When they arrived, Peter withdrew and separated himself [from the Gentiles], fearing them [coming from

James], which were of the circumcision. The other Jews dissembled likewise with him; insomuch that Barnabas also was carried away with their dissimilation. Paul rebuked Peter before them all." (Galatians 2:11–14)

Chapter Seven

Opening the Gates of Heaven on Earth

The New Covenant's Journey to Jerusalem

The chapters previous to Mark's revelation of the forthcoming suffering and death of the "Son of Man" laid the foundation for Jesus's decision to go to Jerusalem. He did not join the disciples, because they carried out his request for them to visit towns and feed the multitudes in the wilderness. He never baptized anyone. He encouraged the disciples to go out on their own to cast out demons and heal those sick. Otherwise they were with him most of the time. They confused their sense of well-being in the company of Jesus with obedience to the Mosaic traditions. They didn't see that the will of God (the Spirit of God) was the driving force in their attachment to Jesus. While they were with Jesus or when they were following his directions, they were feeding on the seed of God sown in them. That seed was the Christ of God, the daily manna fed to their ancestors in the wilderness, reminding them of God's presence and care for them (Galatians 3:16). Left to themselves, as in the boat when the wind was against them, they reverted to the seed of the 'they' world, sown in them from the environment into which they were born (Mark 4:37–40; 6:45–52).

Mark next described Jesus's healing a young boy possessed by a dumb spirit. This was the twelfth healing miracle. The boy's father had brought him to the disciples, but they had not been able to cast out the demon. Jesus explained to them that the spirit was of a kind requiring prayer and fasting (Mark 9:17–29).

Jesus and his disciples began their trek to Jerusalem. Jesus again made the comment, "The Son of man is delivered into the hand of men, and they shall kill him. After his death he would rise on the third day" (Mark 9:31). Jesus then asked the disciples why they disputed among themselves who should be the greatest. Jesus called them together and said, "If any man desires to be first, the same shall be the last of all." He took a child into his arms with the remark, "Whoever shall receive one of such children in my name, receives me and *whoever shall receive me, receives not me, but Him who sent me*" (Mark 9:37). His comment finds its source in Paul's letter to the Romans: "For children, being not yet born, having done neither any evil or good, receive God according to their response to His call of election" (Roman 9:8–11). Mark's intension appears to make his Gospel fit the writings of Paul.

John, the son of Zebedee, raised the question about someone's casting out demons in the name of Jesus, even though he was not a follower of Jesus. Jesus replied with the following remark:

> Forbid them not, for there is no man who shall do a miracle in my name, who can speak lightly of me. For whoever shall give you a cup of water to drink in my name, because you belong to Christ shall not lose his reward. Whoever offends one of these little ones that believe in me, it is better for him if a millstone were hanged about his neck and he was cast into the sea. If your hand, foot or eye offends you, cut it off. It would be better to be without them than be left out of the kingdom of heaven and be cast into unquenchable fire. (Mark 9:39–50)

The unquenchable fire is the chastening of God, which accompanies His continual offer of adoption (Malachi 3:1–3). That offering lies behind Paul's remark about God's care for the well-being of those who trespass off the path of righteousness: "If your enemy hunger, feed him, if he thirst give him drink, for in so doing you shall heap coals of fire on his head" (Romans 12:19f).

As we have already noted, Malachi wrote the messenger of God would sit as a refiner and purifier so that those who trespassed off the path of righteousness could offer unto God an acceptable offering of righteousness (Malachi 3:3).

From Jericho to the Outskirts of Jerusalem

Jesus continued His trek to Jerusalem, moving south on the east side of the Jordan River. Mark's intent was to have Jesus follow the route of the Ark of the Covenant, which crossed the Jordan River under the leadership of Joshua. Mark appears to have intended to picture Jesus's ministry as the background for the development of the New Covenant similar to the establishment of the Old covenant as Paul did (1 Corinthians 10:1–11:28). Pharisees met him on the east side of Jordan and asked if it was lawful for a man to put away his wife. Mark indicated Jesus gave an answer similar to Paul's in 1 Corinthian 7:10–16. Jesus said, "God made them male and female and they shall be one flesh. God hath joined them together, therefore let not man put them asunder" (Mark 10:5–9).

Another man asked Jesus what he should do in order to inherit eternal life. Jesus quoted the commandments to him, which the man said he had observed from his youth. Mark turned to Paul's comment about being crucified and Jesus's answer, which he connected to our being crucified with Christ: "Then Jesus said to him, 'Sell whatever you have and give it to the poor. Take up the cross and follow me.'" The young man grieved, because he had great possessions, which prompted Jesus to say, "It is hard for those who trust in riches to enter into the kingdom of God" (Mark 10:17–31). Paul made a similar statement, warning those with riches not to trust in them. Instead, they should put their trust in God (1 Timothy 6:17). The second letter to Timothy revealed Mark's involvement with Paul and his teaching: "Only Luke is with me. *Take Mark and bring him with you for he is profitable to me for the ministry*" (2 Timothy 4:11). Mark and Luke had an opportunity to share some of their experience with Paul.

Mark next described the time when Jesus addressed his disciples again and elaborated on what things would happen to him:

> We go up to Jerusalem and the Son of man shall be delivered unto the chief priests, and the scribes. They shall scourge him and shall condemn him to death. They shall deliver him to the Gentiles [Romans]. They shall mock him, scourge him, spit upon him and kill him. On the third day he shall rise again. (Mark 10:33f; 14:65)

Mark found his source in Paul's comment, "Christ died for our sins according to scripture. He was buried and rose again according to the scriptures" (1 Corinthians 15:3). In turn, Paul found his source in the prophets Hosea and Isaiah. Hosea wrote of the third-day resurrection while Isaiah wrote of his crucifixion: "He was wounded for our transgressions. With his stripes we are healed. The Lord has laid on him the iniquity of us all. He was oppressed and was afflicted; yet he opened not his mouth. He was brought as a lamb to the slaughter" (Isaiah 53:5). "He gave his back to smiters, and his cheeks to those who plucked off hair. He did not hide his face from shame and spitting" (Isaiah 50:6).

As Jesus continued on his way to Jericho, the two sons of Zebedee asked to be seated on his right and left side when he came into His glory. Jesus asked if they could drink of the cup, to which they replied that they could. Jesus told them it was not his privilege to give the seats they requested. Whoever of the disciples would be chief would be minister and servant of all the disciples, for even the "Son of Man" came not to be ministered to but to minister and give his life as a ransom for many (Mark 10:35–45).

When they came to Jericho, blind Bartimaeus pleaded with Jesus to have mercy on him and to give him his sight. Jesus said, "Go your way. Your faith has made you whole." Immediately, he received his sight and followed Jesus (Mark 10:46–52). It is apparent to me that this thirteenth healing was the last of the purification miracles. Twelve of the thirteen miracles represent the Jews who were purified in anticipation of the inauguration of the New Covenant with Jesus's death and his resurrection in them. The number twelve was really thirteen, because Levi was not included as already demonstrated. Levi represented not only the Jews but also the Gentiles who were yet to be born of God. The thirteenth healing miracle in Jesus' ministry included the Greek mother who shamed Jesus into healing her daughter. But his cleansing of her daughter ws not to be counted like Paul and Mark who were born out of time

The combination of Jew and Gentile falls into place in Paul's letter to the Ephesians:

> You were without Christ of God, being aliens [with regard to the presence of God] from the commonwealth of Israel [Jews], you who were strangers [Gentiles] to the [old] covenants of the promises [made to the Jews], [both] having no hope and without God in this world, now in Christ Jesus [both Jew and Gentile], have our peace. The Christ of God has made both one and has broken down the wall between us…making to himself one new man out of both. Now, both are not strangers and foreigners but fellow citizens of the household of God. You are now built together as a habitation of God through the Spirit. (Ephesians 2:12–22)

The union of Jews and Gentiles in the Christ of God is apparent in his letter to the Romans:

> I beseech you that you present your bodies as a living sacrifice, holy and acceptable to God which is your service to the word, [the Christ of God]. Do not be conformed to this world, but be transformed by the renewing of your mind so that you may prove [for yourselves] what is the good, acceptable, and perfect will of God. We, although being many, are one body in the Christ of God. (Romans 12:1–5)

Isaiah closed his prophecy with a similar statement: "I [God] will gather all nations and tongues. They shall come and see my glory. *I will also make them priests and Levites*" (Isaiah 66:18, 21). We are the Levites who bring forth the will of God, caring for the well-being of the universe, of those near us, and of ourselves. As priests, we sacrifice the selves we have been to take on the life of the Christ of God.

Palm Sunday

When Jesus and his disciples drew near to Jerusalem, Mark cast Jesus in the role of the king of the kingdom of God in keeping with the prophecy of Zechariah: "O daughter of Jerusalem, behold your King comes unto you. He is righteous, and has salvation, riding upon an ass, a colt the foal of an ass" (Zechariah 9:9). Jesus sent his disciples to get such a colt for him to ride into Jerusalem. Some of the crowd spread garments while others cut down branches and strewed them in the way. They went before him and those who followed and cried out, "Hosanna, blessed is the one who comes in the name of the Lord. Blessed be the kingdom of our father David who comes in the name of the Lord" (Mark 11:10).

The celebration of Jesus's entrance into Jerusalem was similar to the celebration given to David when he brought the Ark of the Covenant into Jerusalem. "David and all the house of Israel brought up the ark of the Lord with shouting and the sound of the trumpet" (2 Samuel 6:12-19). At eventide on the day of his arrival, Jesus, with his disciples, entered into the temple to look around. They then went to their lodging in Bethany.

Monday

The next day, according to Mark, they returned to the city. Jesus was hungry, and when he saw a fig tree in the distance, he came to it and looked for fruit. He found only leaves, because it wasn't the time for figs. Jesus said, "Let no man eat of fruit hereafter forever." Jesus was hungry for the fruits of righteousness, which are always in season, especially in Jerusalem. Jesus then went to the temple and began to cast out those who sold and bought in the temple. He overthrew the tables of the money changers and the seats of those who sold doves, quoting Isaiah and Jeremiah, "My house shall be called a house of prayer for all nations, but you have made it a den of thieves" (Mark 11:12–17; Isaiah 56:7; Jeremiah 7:11). At eventide, he left the city.

Mark's description of the cursing of the fig tree and his cleansing of the temple reflect Paul's reference to the prophecy of Hosea. As previously noted, Hosea described how God had torn and slain the Israelites by the prophets. Their priests were like highway robbers. Their fathers, whom God at first had seen as the first fruit of the fig tree, chose to worship Baal-Peor (Hosea: 9:10). It was time to return to God, who would resurrect them to live in His sight through the Christ of God in Jesus.

Tuesday

In the morning as they returned to the city, they saw the fig tree dried from the roots up. The fig tree represented Judaism. No longer would Judaism provide fruits of righteousness by obedience to the law, a strictly Pauline comment. The people themselves would produce the fruits of righteousness as they embraced the New Covenant of the spirit by resurrection from the dead through the cross of Jesus, a Christ of God.

Following Jesus's cursing of the fig tree, Mark described Jesus's address about the forgiveness of God as it came to appear in the Lord's Prayer in the Gospels of Luke and Matthew. Jesus said, "When you pray, forgive, if you hold anything against another so that your Father, who is in heaven may forgive your trespasses" (Mark 11:25). Mark's observation led to Luke and Matthew's development of the Lord's Prayer, as we shall see.

Mark then went on to write the parable about how man killed God's servants and His son when God sent them to retrieve fruits of righteousness from His garden (Mark 12:1–11). Mark tied the story to the scriptural comment: "The stone which the builders rejected had become the head of the corner" (Mark 12:10). Mark's source for this parable was Paul's assurance to the Ephesians: "They are built upon the foundation of the apostles and prophets, Jesus, a Christ of God, being the chief cornerstone in whom you are also built as a habitation of God through the Holy Spirit" (Ephesians 2:19–22). Again, we find that this parable could not have been said by Jesus, because Jesus was a follower of John the Baptist for the most part and would not have seen God taking habitation in a human.

Pharisees continued to pressure Jesus about his teaching, asking him whether it was lawful to render tribute to Caesar or not. Jesus took note of Caesar's image on the coins and answered, "Render to Caesar things that are Caesar's and to God the things that are God's" (Mark

12:13–17). Paul addressed the same issue in his letter to the Romans: "Rulers are not a terror to good works, but to evil. Render therefore all their dues: tribute to whom tribute is due. Owe no man any thing but to love one another; for love fulfills the law" (Romans 13:1–8).

Mark next gave warnings as to what to expect under the circumstances of the persecution of Christians. First of all, Jesus warned them to take heed lest they be deceived by anyone claiming to be Christ. Jesus's warning was similar to Paul's caution, which he gave to the Galatians: "There be some that trouble you and would pervert the Gospel of Christ. If anyone preaches a Gospel other than what you have received from me, let him be accursed" (Galatians 1: 6–9).

Mark continued his warning of what the Christians would face (Mark 13:9–13). He wrote that they would be delivered up to councils. In the synagogues, they would be beaten. They would be brought before rulers and kings for Christ's sake. Brother would betray brother, and the father, son. Children would rise up against parents and cause put them to death. They should watch for they would not know when the master of the house (God) would be coming (Mark 13:5–36).

Wednesday

The chief priests and the scribes sought how they might take hold of Jesus and put him to death. Meanwhile, a woman came and poured an expensive ointment on Jesus's head, which upset the disciples, for it was a waste of money. Jesus spoke of her gift as an anointing of *his body for its burial.* Judas then went to the high priests to betray him (Mark 14:1–11).

Thursday

Jesus began the day by sending two of the disciples to make arrangements for celebration of the Passover that evening, which would mark the beginning of Good Friday. At the Last Supper, Mark described Jesus's reiteration of the words about the bread and wine revealed to Paul by God.

Mark described the capture of Jesus at the hands of the temple hierarchy. All the disciples abandoned him except Peter, who followed after Jesus only to deny him as the high priest took witness against Jesus. In the morning, they took Jesus to Pilate. The story from there on is well-known and needs no repetition. However, it is worthwhile to review some of the details, which find their source in the Old Testament.

Peter followed Jesus into the palace of the high priest and sat with the servants. Many gave false witness against Jesus. Jesus acknowledged that he was the Christ, the Son of God. Some began to spit on him, and servants struck him with the palm of their hands. A servant accused Peter of being a follower of Jesus. Peter's first denial marked the first day, and the first cockcrow followed, marking the beginning of the second day. Peter's second denial was followed by the second cockcrow, marking the beginning of the third day. Peter's vehement third denial brought Jesus's earlier statement about the cock crowing to Peter's mind. "When Peter thought thereon, he wept." It appears to me that he shed tears of purification, heralding his being raised from the dead after three days (Mark 14:30, 66–70).

The kiss Judas gave to Jesus to identify him to the soldiers of the high priest reflected the words of Psalm 2: "The kings and rulers take council against God's Christ. Kiss the son, lest God be angry and you perish on the way" (Psalm 2:1–12).

The chief priests accused Jesus of many things, but he answered nothing. Pilate marveled at Jesus's silence when Pilate asked if he was the king of the Jews (Mark 15:2–3). In this regard, Isaiah wrote the following:

> He is despised and rejected, a man of sorrows, and acquainted with grief … He was wounded for our transgressions and with his stripes we are healed. The Lord has laid upon him the iniquity of us all. He was afflicted yet he opened not his mouth. He was brought as a lamb to the slaughter. He has poured out his soul; my righteous servant justified many. He was numbered with transgressors and made intercession for them. (Isaiah 53:3–12)

Mark outlined the wounds Jesus suffered in the description of his scourging at the hands of the soldiers. They clothed him with purple and platted a crown of thorns, which they put on his head (Mark 15:2,

9, 17). They smote him with a reed, spat on him, and bowed their knees in mock worship of him (Mark 15:15–19; Isaiah 50:6). They pierced his hands and his feet (Luke 24:39; Psalm 22:16). They parted his garments and cast lots to determine what each man should take from him (Mark 15:24; Psalm 22:18). The transgressors with whom Jesus numbered and made intercession were the two thieves crucified with Jesus, which was noted to be the fulfillment of the scriptural statement (Mark 15:28; Isaiah 53:12).

In the sixth hour, there was darkness over the land. When the ninth hour arrived—in keeping with Isaiah's prophecy—darkness covered the earth until the Lord God arose upon the people and His glory was seen upon them (Mark 15:33; Isaiah 60:2; Zephaniah 1:15). At the ninth hour, Jesus cried with a loud voice, "My God, my God, why have you forsaken me?" (Mark 15:34; Psalm 22:1). His cry prompted one standing by to run and fill a sponge full of vinegar for Jesus to drink (Mark 15:36, Psalm 69:21). Jesus thereupon gave up his spirit.

Joseph of Arimathaea, a wealthy member of the Sanhedrim and a disciple of Jesus, got Pilate's permission to put Jesus's body in a sepulcher hewn out of rock. As predicted by Isaiah, "God's servant made his grave with the rich in his death" (Isaiah 53:9; Mark 15:43).

According to Mark, on the morning after the Sabbath, women went to the sepulcher to prepare Jesus's body for its burial, but they found the tomb empty. A young man told them to tell the disciples that Jesus had gone before them to Galilee and that they would find him there. The women were afraid and did not tell anyone among them. The other three Gospels tell of differing occasions when Jesus appeared to the disciples in Jerusalem and later in Galilee. Paul lists Jesus's appearances according to what he received:

> I delivered unto you how Christ died for our sins according to the scriptures, how *he was buried*, and rose again on the third day according to the Scriptures. He appeared first unto Peter, then to the twelve. After that he was seen by above five hundred brethren at once, and then unto James [Jesus's brother] followed by all the apostles. Last of all he was seen of me, as of one born out of time. I am the least of all the apostles because I persecuted the Church of God. But, I am what I am

by the grace of God [the gift of the Christ of God]. I labored more than all the others; yet [it was not] not I, but [it was] the grace of God which was with me. (1 Corinthians 15:1–10)

Mark wrote his Gospel around AD 66 to AD 70, a time of chaos throughout the Roman Empire. Nero set fire to Rome in AD 64. He blamed the Christians and issued an edict ordering their punishment throughout the empire. His edict was carried out haphazardly. Persecution of the Christians depended on complaints raised by Jews in areas where the Christians had made roads into Judaism. It is possible that Paul was one of the first to be put to death, because he was under house arrest in Rome, awaiting audience before Nero. During this period of persecution, Christians used the sign of a fish to identify themselves to other Christians. The letters of the word for fish were the initial letters of the words "Jesus, Christ, God, son, savior" (Wikipedia, Title: The History of the Christian Fish Symbol).

The situation in Jerusalem first began to come apart under newly appointed procurators in AD 62 and AD 64. Their general corruption and ruthless mismanagement roused the population to armed resistance against Rome. Nero's burning of Rome put the whole empire in a state of concern, which ultimately led to the death of Nero in AD 68. The chaos in Rome stirred the Judean population to rebel against Roman occupation of their territories. By AD 66, Israelites had taken control of Judea. However, the various parties in Judaism fought with one another to gain control of sections of the country and of Jerusalem itself. The zealots took control of the area outside the temple, while the priestly hierarchy continued to control the worship area inside the temple itself (Noth 1958, 438).

According to the historian Josephus, at the urging of the priestly hierarchy, the Roman Procurator ordered James, and possibly Peter also, to be stoned to death in AD 62. This led the religious community of "the People of the Way" to flee to the city of Pella, which was northeast of the Sea of Galilee.

Mark introduced an anachronism when Jesus called the first disciple to join his fishing for men. A second anachronism showed up in the food available to feed the five thousand at the first feeding of the multitudes. The two small fish and the five loaves of bread available during the first feeding might have represented Peter and Paul. Paul wrote of their designation for these roles in his letter to the Galatians, fourteen years after his first missionary journey. False Jerusalem brethren had spied on him to prove he and Barnabas were enemies of the followers of John the Baptist. Paul and Barnabas came to Jerusalem and met with the pillars of the Jerusalem fellowship, namely James (Jesus's brother), Peter, and John, who was a son of Zebedees. The three pillars gave Paul and Barnabas the right hands of fellowship, agreeing that Paul and Barnabas should "go unto the heathen and they [the People of the Way] unto the circumcision" under Peter (Galatians 2:1–9).

Paul's description of the appearance of Christ in him on the road to Damascus is applicable to the faithful readers of his epistles:

> I knew a man in Christ more than fourteen years ago, whether in the body or out of the body, I cannot tell, who was caught up to the third heaven. He was caught into paradise [heaven] and heard unspeakable words. There was a thorn given to me according to the flesh. I besought the Lord to take it away and he said to me, "My grace is sufficient for you, for my strength is perfected in weakness." Since you seek a proof of Christ speaking in me, examine yourselves. Don't you know your own selves, how Jesus, a Christ of God, is in you? Examine yourselves. (2 Corinthians 12:1–9; 13:5)

As Christians, we are called to be the messengers of the New Covenant. We turn our lives over to the life of God. Entrusting ourselves to God, we become the expression of His word in our flesh. We join with Jesus, Paul, Peter, and the other writers of the New Testament as instruments of God's reconciling the world to Himself. We are not God any more than they were. The life of God emanates from inside our being to stimulate the seeds of God in those nearby, priming them to choose the carefulness of God.

Paul's understanding of the Gospel of God was based on God's presence in our lives. God interfaced with us through the carefulness of the high road. Paul summed up his image of life as a Christ of God in his statement, "All who are led by the spirit of God is an offspring of

God by the spirit of adoption whereby we cry, 'Abba, Father'" (Romans 8:14).

So far we have traced the development of the image of our lives as Christs of God, starting with the four Gospels' dependence on the writings of St. Paul. We have seen how his writings traced their source to the writings of the Old Testament. Paul's source for calling God "Father" appeared in the Eden story, in which God formed man out of clay and then breathed His spirit into man, making him a living soul. The significance of this beginning is Adam's transformation to be a Christ of God. Adam was the progenitor of the human race, so the caring dimension of the Christ of God was seeded in every human being.

Jesus was totally human. He inherited the seed of God just as others before him, such as Moses, Samuel, Saul, David, and Cyrus of Persia, were filled with the spirit of God. If you knew where Jesus was buried, you would find his bones. According to Paul, Jesus was buried (1 Corinthians 15:4). Jesus committed only his spirit into the hands of God as he died on the cross (Luke 23:46). The spirit of God—God's expression of Himself as His word—came upon the prophets, especially to Isaiah. The presence of the Christ of God in Jesus's disciples and his followers was the same as in Jesus. Every human receives an option to be born of God. It would not matter whether a person ever heard the Gospel or believed that Jesus was the son of God.

But there is a catch to being Christian. Our commitment to the life of God has to come from the heart. We have to be "as a chaste virgin" (2 Corinthians 11:2) to be the temple where God dwells. It sounds like an oxymoron, but the truth is that we can't become the children of God in order to be the children of God. Helping others cannot be payment for an insurance policy. Living the life of God is not protection from accidents, catastrophes, and sicknesses. Luke made that point in his description of Jesus's comments. There is no benefit of living the life of God except the sense of fulfillment, but we have to be careful. If we do it because it makes us feel better, we aren't living the life of God, We have slipped back into the uncaring 'they' world. "Do you think those eighteen upon whom the tower of Siloam fell and killed them were sinners above all who lived in Jerusalem (Luke 13:4)?" We are only thinking of ourselves if we choose the high road of carefulness because those who are caring live longer on the high road and are healthier than those on the low road of carelessness.

If the Gospels and the writings of Paul are about the Christ of God, what do we know about the life of Jesus? His baptism, his leadership of the followers of John the Baptist, his overpowering charisma, which had a cleansing effect on those who sought him out, his dedication to preaching of a heartfelt obedience to the law and commandments, his sensitivity to those around him, his concern for the materialism of Judaism, his anticipation of the establishment of the kingdom of God as a benevolent society based on faith in God's concern, not unlike the a father has for his children's welfare, his sense of confrontation with the political and religious structure, his crucifixion—all of these stand out in the Gospels.

The preaching and writings of St. Paul were based on his knowledge of the Old Testament and his experience on the road to Damascus. He recognized his experience was a fulfillment of the prophecies and promises of the Old Testament. God would reveal His presence in mankind and would establish a New Covenant. Paul also recognized that Jesus was leading "the People of the Way" in the way of righteousness without their understanding of what was happening to them. They were unlearned and ignorant (Acts 4:13). Unlearned meant they knew little about the Bible, and ignorant meant that they could not read or write.

Paul wrote his epistles from about AD 50 to AD 60. The Gospels were written from about AD 66 to AD 95. The first three Gospels cover about one year of Jesus's preaching, while John's Gospel covers a period of three years, judging by the number of times Jesus observed the feast of the Passover in each Gospel. The only other history of Jesus's ministry comes from Josephus, who wrote in AD 80, copying what was said in the New Testament.

The Gospels intertwined the preaching, writings and experiences of St. Paul into the details of Jesus's life. Mark led the way, because he could read and write. He was also a protégé of Paul, and he was the son of a family in whose house the Jerusalem community of "the People of the Way" gathered. He, too, like Paul, studied the Bible under a sage like Gamaliel, if not Gamaliel himself. St. Paul and Mark were the right persons in the right place at the right time.

The Fellowship of the Saints in Christ

The Jerusalem community developed three to five years after the crucifixion. In Paul's letters, he admits to persecuting the Jerusalem community, which called themselves "the People of the Way." They continued to follow the John the Baptist's way of righteousness by obedience to the law. At the same time, Peter and Stephan (Acts7:51f) recognized Jesus was the prophet whom God had promised to raise from the midst of Israel (Deuteronomy 18:15–18). The prophet would be like Moses, it was said. God would put His words into the prophet's mouth to speak to the people. Peter declared the following to a crowd in Jerusalem:

> The God of Abraham, Isaac and Jacob has glorified His Son, Jesus, whom you have delivered up and rejected him in the presence of Pilate, when he was determined to let him go. You denied the Holy One and the Just, and desired a murderer to be granted unto you. [You] killed the Prince of Life whom God had raised from the dead. Repent therefore and be converted so that your sins may be blotted out, when the times of refreshing shall come from the presence of the Lord. He shall send Jesus, a Christ of God, whom the heaven must receive until the time of restitution. Moses truly said unto the fathers, 'A prophet shall the Lord God raise up unto you. (Acts' 3:12–26; Deuteronomy 15)

Stephen made the same declaration about the people's killing of Jesus, "the Just One":

> Moses said to the children of Israel: A prophet shall the Lord your God raise up to your brethren. Listen to him. You stiff-necked and uncircumcised in your heart and ears, you have always resisted the Holy Spirit, as your fathers did. Which of the prophets have your fathers not persecuted? They have slain them who revealed the Just One [Jesus] of whom you have now been the betrayers and murderers. (Acts 7:51)

Before the crowd stoned Stephan, they laid down their clothes at a young man's feet named Saul (later known as Paul) and who consented to the execution. The reference to Paul as a young man meant that he was about eighteen to twenty-one years old. His consent indicated he had some representation on the Sanhedrin or on a committee of the Sanhedrin.

The Book of Acts began with the ending of Luke's Gospel. According to Luke, the disciples remained in Jerusalem after Jesus's crucifixion unlike the other writers of the New Testament. Luke's Gospel ended with Jesus telling the disciples to "tarry in the city until they were endued with power from on high." When he blessed them, Jesus was parted from them and was carried up to heaven. Jesus told them they should not depart from Jerusalem until they received the Holy Spirit (Acts1:5–8). At the feast of Pentecost, the sound of a rushing wind filled the house where the apostles were gathered. They were filled with the Holy Spirit and spoke in tongues.

"The People of the Way" believed Jesus was the only Christ. The Christ of God was now in them, while the spirit of Jesus was in heaven, sitting on the right hand of God. They didn't understand the Holy Spirit had raised them from the dead to live the life of God. They probably attributed their sense of fulfillment of their destiny to obedience of the law. As we have seen in reviewing Mark's Gospel, the disciples never did understand what Jesus meant when he said that he would be put death and would rise from the dead three days later.

Their way of thinking meant they followed the law and commandments from their hearts. I think there was one thing of the provisions of the law they ignored. John's baptism meant repentance for the forgiveness of sin. There was no need for them to pay for a sin with sacrifice. *Paul* saw this as disobedience of the law. For a year or two after Stephen's death, Paul persecuted "the People of the Way." Many of them fled from Jerusalem to Assyria and the Decapolis cities. Paul decided to take his persecution to Damascus and even got a letter from the high priest authorizing him to do so.

As we have already seen, the trip to Damascus would have taken about six or seven days. Paul probably spent most of his time developing a presentation for the leaders of the synagogues so that he could persuade them to give him the names of "the People of the Way." He would have been reviewing his knowledge of scripture, reviewing the leading prophets like Hosea, Isaiah, Jeremiah, and Malachi. He would be talking to himself and to God, too.

Overview of the One God

The list of the similarities of the life and sayings of Paul and Jesus in Mark's Gospel, Section "The New Imitates the Old" of Chapter Four, kept bothering me. I am now convinced that Mark intentionally wrote the beginning of the Gospel of Christ as the life and preaching of St. Paul's ministry and not Jesus's. Jesus predicted his forthcoming crucifixion and his resurrection three times (Mark 98:31; 9:31; 10:33). Such a statement would take the heart out of his suffering and death. How could his death be a sacrifice if he knew he would be resurrected three days after his suffering and crucifixion? Furthermore Jesus's suffering was for a shorter time compared to Paul's suffering, which was equal, if not more than Jesus's. Paul wrote the following:

> Of the Jews, five times I received forty stripes save one. Thrice I was beaten with rods, once I was stoned, thrice I suffered shipwreck, a night and a day I have been in the ocean. In journeys often, in perils of waters, in perils of robbers, in perils by mine own countrymen, in perils by the heathen, in perils in the city, in perils in the wilderness, in perils in the sea, in perils among false brethren, in weariness, and painfulness, in watchings often, in hunger and thirst, in fastings often, in cold and naked. (2 Corinthians11:21–27)

Jesus's statement about death and resurrection could not have been said by Jesus. Mark's Gospel was based on the life of Paul. Mark indicated he was going to write about the beginning of the Gospel of Jesus Christ. Mark was referring to life and writings of St. Paul. Without Paul's understanding, there would be no message about the meaning and significance of Jesus's life. Paul indicated that his source was the writings of the prophets. In reviewing the Gospel of St. Mark, we have seen how Mark relied on Paul and the prophets. The remark about Jesus's death and resurrection could only be the made by Paul.

Why does Mark indicate he was writing about the Gospel of Jesus? He could do this because Paul was a Christ of God just as Jesus was a Christ of God.

The prophets were also Christs of God even though they didn't recognize themselves as such. The expressional Word of God, the Spirit of God, was upon them. Isaiah was specific in his declaration that the "the Spirit of God was upon him, because the Lord God had anointed (Septuagint, 'christed') me to preach the gospel (Septuagint 'good tidings', Isaiah 61:1). When we are alive from the dead in Christ, our members—arms, lips, ear, eyes, etc.—are instruments of righteousness unto God (Romans 6:13). There could only be one Christ, because there is only one God.

> You are the Body of Christ. (Romans 12:27)

> As the body is one and has many members, all the members of that one body,, although they are many, are one body, so is Christ. By one Spirit we are all baptized into one body. The members of the body are equally important. (1 Corinthians 12:11f; 25)

> (God) has delivered us from the power of darkness and translated us into the kingdom of his offspring in whom we have redemption through his blood, the forgiveness of sin, and who is the image of the invisible God. He is the head of the body; he takes preeminence in all things. (Colossians 1:13–15; 18)

> Christ is the head corner stone. (Psalm 118:22; Mark 12:10; Ephesians 2:20)

When Paul came in sight of Damascus, the light of understanding the dead life he had been living under the law and commandments blinded him. It may be he was disappointed with the way the hierarchy was running the temple worship by taking advantage of the worshippers. Perhaps, the thorns that he felt may have included the inconsistencies between the law and the prophets that he discovered in his studies in

Jerusalem. He probably felt guilt about consenting to the stoning of Stephen. He realized he had been fighting the burs and thorns of God's chastening. He committed himself to the hands of God and sought out baptism. He joined himself to the People of the Way. God revealed the son in him (Galatians 1:16).

The description of the stoning of Stephen as Paul came to understand it, according to the Book of Acts, is anachronistic, which is true of most of Acts prior to Paul's Damascus experience. Luke joined with Paul in his third missionary journey. During this time Paul must have explained to him in more detail what transpired on the Damascus Road. The critical statement of Stephen, which led to his death, was probably his comment, "Which of the prophets have not your fathers persecuted and they have slain them "who showed before (in the past of Scripture) of the coming of the Just (Righteous) One" (Acts 7:52). That statement in itself would have been sufficient to stir the crowd to stone Stephen. To them, a Greek convert of the gates had no right to quote scripture about their fathers' killing of the prophets. The early People of the Way spoke of Jesus as a prophet while Paul recognized an important statement about *the Righteous One* in the Book of Deuteronomy, not mentioned by Stephen or Peter. The book of Deuteronomy indicated that the Righteous One of would be a prophet "like unto Moses" (Deuteronomy 18:15). The likeness between Moses and Jesus was more than both setting the people free from bondage to the Egyptians for Moses and from the sin of the law as the measurement of Righteousness for Jesus. The likeness was that they both established a Covenant, the Covenant of the law for Moses written in concrete and the New Covenant of the Holy Spirit dwelling in the people. The latter displaced the Covenant of the law for the covenant with God himself dwelling in the temple of our bodies. Luke described Paul's experience as an inner voice which said to him, "Paul, why do your persecute me? I am Jesus, whom you are persecuting. It is hard to for you to kick against the thorns" (Acts 9:4f).

Paul's world broke into pieces. He saw that his obsession for obedience to all of the law, which required a sacrificial atonement for breaking the law as opposed to being baptized for the remission of sin embraced by the People of the Way, led to his persecution of them for breaking the law. Paul experienced God's forgiveness for his persecuting people who were obeying the law from their hearts and not by their following in the footsteps of Jesus with realizing that the latter was their reason for feeling free from sin.

Paul couldn't help but think of Jermiah's declaration of a new covenant wherein God "would put the law in their hearts for they would know the Lord God from the least to the greatest." God would forgive their iniquity and would no longer remember their sin. The New Covenant turned not to the temple or the priestly hierarchy but to the individual people who would know God in themselves (Jeremiah still held to the Law. (Jeremiah 31:31-34)

In the desert Paul found himself thinking about Isaiah's prophecies, which we discussed in previous pages, showing how the Holy Spirit was the gift of the life of God emanating from the heart of being as God was and how God would send His servant, who would be the covenant of the spirit, to die as a propitiation for sin through faith in the blood of his life (Romans 3:25). Then Paul connected to Malachi's prophecies that God was going to send two messengers, one of whom himself he would be the covenant, and one whom, according to Isaiah (53:6), God would lay the iniquity of all. Luke's description of Stephen's speech made reference to Jesus as the Righteous prophet of the Book of Deuteronomy in his comment that his listeners had been the betrayers and murders of the Righteousness One of Deuteronomy.

The entwinement of these prophecies could only be made by someone like Paul, not just because of his familiarity with Holy Scripture , but especially because of his experience of these events on the road to Damascus. Luke became privy to Paul's thinking through Luke's close accompaniment with him on his third missionary journey and trip to Rome, enabling Luke to write about Stephen as he did.

The best image of how those pieces fitted together is found in the Twenty-Third Psalm, which is so close to Paul's preaching it probably led him to understand what it meant to be a Christ of God. The Twenty-Third Psalm has given comfort from the time it was written somewhere between three hundred and nine hundred years before the birth of Jesus and before Paul's understanding about what it meant to be a child of God:

The Lord is my Shepherd; I shall not want.
*He provides me with all I need, physically and spiritually,
to be a child of God.*

He maketh me to lie down in green pastures.
He leadeth me beside still waters.
He satisfies my hunger and thirst

He restoreth my soul.
He leadeth me in the paths of righteousness for His name's sake.
*He leads me back to the path of righteousness if I trespass
into the 'they' world.*

Yea, though I walk through valley of the shadow of death, I will fear no evil,
For thou art with me; thy rod and thy staff they comfort me.
*You have dressed me with truth girt around my loins,
the breastplate of righteousness, the footwear of the* Gospel
*of peace, the shield of faith, the helmet of salvation, and
the sword of the spirit, which is the word of God. Your
chastening strengthens my faith.* (Ephesians 6:11–17;
Psalm 18:32)

Thou preparest a table before me in the presence of my enemies.
Thou anointest my head with oil; my cup runneth over.
*You deck your altar for me with the daily manna-bread so
I may feed on your presence. You heal me with the blood
of your life so the fullness of your being may flow in my
veins.*

> Surely goodness and mercy shall follow me all the days
> of my life;
> And I will dwell in the house of the Lord forever.
> *Goodness and mercy shall spread out behind me like the*
> *wake of a ship. I will be your temple for you to live in me*
> *and for me to live in you.*

The Twenty-Third Psalm, together with the Lord's Prayer, provide us with the means of keeping us aware of the presence of God in our daily living. When we wake in the morning, we usually find ourselves imaging what we have to do for the day. Either of these can be said in less than a minute. Doing so brings God into the picture of the day's activities ahead of us. The Psalm is a good way to begin the day, while the Lord's Prayer works well when we fall into bed at night. During the day, if we should feel we are loosing control of ourself because of some frustration or argument, we can stimulate the seed of God within us by saying, "Can you give me a hand here, God?"

Choosing to live the life of God on a day to day basis is not easy. It takes commitment which can be strengthened by our association with like minded people in prayer, thanksgiving, study of Scripture and feeding on the presence of Christ in those around in one another. Such involvement with one another is the best way to fulfill Paul's hope for us when he wrote:

> May God grant you, according to the riches of His glory, to be strengthened with might by His Spirit in the inner man. May the Christ of God dwell in your hearts by faith so you, being rooted and grounded in love, may be able to comprehend with all the saints what is the breadth and length and depth and height of the love of the Christ of God and *be filled with all the fullness of God. Unto Him, who is able to do exceeding abundantly above all we ask or think, according to the power which works in us, be glory in the church by the Christ of God in Jesus, worlds without end. Amen.* (Ephesians 3:16–21)

Postscript

This postscript about the abstraction of the Gospel message in the words of the Twenty-Third Psalm comes to you with some trepidation on my part. It is my response to an editor's suggestion: "If it's your own work, please tell the reader about when you wrote it." At first, I was very reluctant, but it stuck on my mind, and I began to think how I came to include the Twenty-Third Psalm. I am not a very sensitive person, but as I thought about it a few tears came to my eyes.

As I started to think about when this abstraction developed, I remembered that I had done a similar abstraction of the Lord's Prayer at the funeral of a friend of mine earlier this year, which I incorporated above in this book. After the service, a few people asked for copies of what I had said. Later, on the way home, it occurred to me that I had made a similar short abstraction about "goodness and mercy's following me all the days of my life like the wake of a ship" in a much earlier sermon two years ago, which included Micah's statement that what the Lord expects of us is the following: "To show mercy, to live righteously and to walk humbly with your God" (Micah 6:8). It probably came to mind because after that sermon a few people commented about how they liked that abstraction. And they asked for copies.

The bow wake of a ship gets broader and broader as it spreads across the ocean, encompassing more area just as goodness (godliness) and mercy increase as it spreads out touching more and more people for them to live the life of God. In the rest of the drive home, thoughts kept running through my mind about the words of the whole psalm.

I felt overwhelmed to see how close they summarized Paul's Gospel of God in this book.

—G. W. Cummings

Bibliography

Andersen, Bernhard W. *Understanding the Old Testament.* Englewood, NJ: Prentice Hall, 1975.

Brenton, Lancelot. *The Septuagint with Apocrypha: Greek and English.* Peabody, MA: Hendrickson Publishers, 1992.

Cummings, George W. *What Ever Happened to Levi?* Alhambra, CA: Canon Press, 2002.

Goleman, Daniel. *Social Intelligence.* New York: Bantam Book, 2007.

Heidegger, Martin. *Being and Time.* London: Camelot Press, 1962.

Isaacson, Walter. *Einstein: His Life and Universe.* New York: Simon & Shuster, 2008.

Magee, Bryan. *The Story of Philosophy.* New York: DK Publishing, 2001.

Noth, Martin. *The History of Israel.* New York: Harper and Row, 1958.

Nestle, Eberhard. *Novum Testamentum Graece.* Stuttgart, Germany: Privileg, Wurtz, Bibelanstalt.

Safrai, S, and M. Stern, eds. *The Jewish People in the First Century.* Philadelphia: Fortress Press, 1976.

Smith, Anthony. *Intimate Universe: The Human Body*. New York: Random House, 1998.

Strong, James. *The Strongest Strong's Exhaustive Concordance to the Bible*. Grand Rapids, MI: Zondervan, 1975.

Also by George Cummings

Theophilus, 1969, Canon Press, San Marino, California.

For The Love of God, 1992, Canon Press Pasadena, California.

Born of God, 1994, Canon Press, Pasadena, California.

Whatever Happened to Levi, Canon Press 2002, Pasadena, California.

Understanding the Message, 2007, Cathedral Center Press, Los Angeles, California.